Administrative and Business Communication

ADMINISTRATIVE AND BUSINESS COMMUNICATION

ARVIND KUMAR BHATT
PhD, MBA, MCA, HDTE

Expatriate Consultant
Department of Management,
School of Business & Management
Addis Ababa Science & Technology University
Federal Democratic Republic of Ethiopia

LAXMI PUBLICATIONS (P) LTD.
(An ISO 9001:2008 Company)
BENGALURU • CHENNAI • COCHIN • GUWAHATI • HYDERABAD
JALANDHAR • KOLKATA • LUCKNOW • MUMBAI • RANCHI • NEW DELHI
BOSTON (USA) • ACCRA (GHANA) • NAIROBI (KENYA)

ADMINISTRATIVE AND BUSINESS COMMUNICATION

Printed and bound in India
Typeset at Shubham Composer, Delhi
First Edition : 2015
ISBN 978-93-83828-51-7

Branches

Bengaluru	080-26 75 69 30	
Chennai	044-24 34 47 26,	24 35 95 07
Cochin	0484-237 70 04,	405 13 03
Guwahati	0361-254 36 69,	251 38 81
Hyderabad	040-27 55 53 83,	27 55 53 93
Jalandhar	0181-222 12 72	
Kolkata	033-22 27 43 84	
Lucknow	0522-220 99 16	
Mumbai	022-24 91 54 15,	24 92 78 69
Ranchi	0651-220 44 64	

PUBLISHED IN INDIA BY

Laxmi Publications (P) Ltd.
(An ISO 9001:2008 Company)
113, GOLDEN HOUSE, DARYAGANJ,
NEW DELHI - 110002, INDIA
Telephone : 91-11-4353 2500, 4353 2501
Fax : 91-11-2325 2572, 4353 2528
www.laxmipublications.com
info@laxmipublications.com

C—
Printed at : Repro Knowledgecast Limited, Thane

Dedicated

To

my respected father

Late Shri Ganga Ram Bhatt

His blessing is always with us

to follow the pathway of

success and enlightenment........

Foreword by Dr. Tarekegn Tadesse Tanga

Greetings for the knowledge creation!

It's a great pleasure for me to write this foreword letter for the book written by Dr. Arvind Kumar Bhatt; an iconic academician in the field of Business and Management.

Business Communication methods have been transforming the work culture of the organizations day by day. The need for communication skills is important in virtually every career, not just those that are traditionally regarded as people-oriented. Practitioners in organizations spend their maximum time in communicating with others, individually and in groups. Likewise, engineers spend most of their professional lives in writing, speaking and listening. Technical people with good communication skills earn more, and those who are weak communicators suffer. William Schaffer, International business development manager for Sun Microsystems, made the point emphatically: "If there's one skill that's required for success in this industry, it's communication skill." Other high-tech experts back up this claim. Over 90% of the personnel officials at 500 US businesses stated that increased communication skills are needed for success in the 21st century.

This book **"Administrative and Business Communication"** will help students to get deep insight of communication and as well as prepare themself for the organization in this global competitive environment. I congratulate Dr. Arvind Kumar Bhatt on his efforts to bring this book and wish him all the best for future endeavour.

Dr. Tarekegn Tadesse Tanga
President
Addis Ababa Science & Technology University
Addis Ababa, Ethiopia

Foreword by Dugassa Mulugeta

At all levels of development in human activities, Communication is one of the most important instruments to make any transactions between two or more people. Leave alone human beings, even animals instinctively communicate with each other for various reasons. Therefore, communication is the vital element among human beings in their day-to-day life.

In modern society of industrial and information technology, communication becomes a very powerful instrument that individuals must acquire to be able to perform their duties and responsibilities, and become efficient managers and/or effective leaders in this dynamic business world, the world of globalization.

In this regard, the book "Administrative and Business Communication" written by Dr. Arvind K. Bhatt, contributes a lot to the area of communication where individuals, businessmen, teachers, students, researchers and others develop good communication skills to impart information in different ways to achieve the desired goals.

Dugassa Mulugeta (PhD)
Dean, School of Business & Management
Addis Ababa Science & Technology University
Addis Ababa, Ethiopia

Foreword by Professor D.P. Sharma

Congratulations! It's a great pleasure for me to write this foreword letter for the book "Administrative & Business Communication" written by Dr. Arvind Kumar Bhatt; a well-known Management scholar and corporate trainer in the field of Business and Management practices. Communication skills are vital for success endeavours of any professional. Management and Business Communication processes have been changing with rapid speed in techno-global environment. Technological Communication is a new horizon where technology is enforcing the Business & Management practices to change their communication climate. This book is the true outcome of the thrust for changes in paradigms of communication engineering. If we have a close look on the contents of the book, we will find that, it has dealt with the important basics of communication with convergence of technology based tools and techniques. The book briefly covers the advancements in communication technologies, and developments of communication systems especially in developing countries like India. Further, it covers detailed elements of Media of Communication like Oral Communication, Speech, Telephoning, face to face conversation, Active listening, Interviews, Meetings and Written Communication including Business letter writing, Memo and Report Writing. It explains how these communication styles and mechanisms can be supported by modern tools and technologies especially in information and communication technologies in organization communication cultures.

Overall, there are no hard and fast rules to make strong communication skills, so there's room to be creative and have fun with communication and skills! As a final note the book is a true knowledge bank for communication skills.

Dr. D.P. Sharma
Professor
Computer Science & IT
http://dpsharma.info

Foreword by Professor T.K. Jain

Administrative and Business Communication plays a very important role in the development of business environment. Communication plays a very important role in the development of any business organization or business environment in the country at large. It protocols help in the development of business environment. Dr. Arvind Bhatt has carried out a comprehensive study on this domain and has brought out this useful academic contribution, which is primarily to serve the business community and the management graduates. He has addressed a very important issue. This book will bridge the vacuum and help the academic community tremendously in meeting the requirements of the emerging business leaders. The readers are fortunate that the tremendous efforts of Dr. Bhatt are presented in this book for their studies and learning. I thank Dr. Bhatt for this amazing masterpiece venture.

Trilok Kumar Jain

Dean

International School of Business Management

Jaipur

Foreword by Himanshu Sharma

I was very delighted and honoured when Dr. Arvind Bhatt asked me to write a few lines for foreword section in his new textbook. He is known by his great achievements in his field of studies and contribution to society by his hard work. Since I have been knowing him for decades, I must say that the efforts he put while authoring this textbook are commendable.

My specialisation is Management Information Systems (MIS). Effective communication of information plays a significant role in implementing MIS. I strongly believe that this textbook could be very helpful for the readers who are studying business communication skills as a prerequisite for courses like MIS or related subjects. This textbook is a mine of information with simple and useful illustrations.

Lastly, this book is unique and surely a treasure for people exploring effective techniques of communication skills in organizations. Thank you Arvind for producing such a masterpiece of work.

Himanshu Sharma
(Lecturer)
Information Technology Department
Nizwa College of Technology
Ministry of Manpower
Sultanate of Oman

Preface

Communication skills are essential in any domain of human interaction. In fact, when all is said and done, on whatever level, communication is the sole activity that all people share. The benefits of effective communication are too numerous to mention, but they enhance all aspects of life from personal to professional. The ability to communicate is vital to the success of any endeavour.

Business Communication is the process of transmission of information within the business environment and the quality of communication directly influences the success of any business. In today's business practices information is passed to the employees regarding the organization's objectives, job instructions for the employees at all the levels of the organization, customer orders, production-related problems, employee related issues like employees' recognition, promotion, complaints and many other issues are the important information exchanged among the employees of the organizations.

Communication skills are also required for the executives in the organizations in order to make speeches, prepare pamphlets, brochures, souvenirs and making announcement into media to project a favourable image about their company. An improved communication skill benefits both the employee and the organization. Skilled employees become an asset for themselves as well as for the organization.

Due to advancement in communication technologies, there are remarkable developments of communication system. With the help of these tools and technologies communication becomes instantaneous and more effective than ever before. The advanced technology of mass media and telecommunication has attracted the attention of the business organizations in many fields. The technology, skills of using media and some concepts of communication are useful to overcome from some of the communication barriers.

This book is developed and designed for the undergraduate and master's program students of various universities in Ethiopia and India. This book is presented into two parts; the first part of the book has six chapters. In this part students will go through the important basics of communication in chapters and also technology based tools and techniques used for business communication by the organizations and its impact.

The second part has eight chapters which cover the detailed elements of Media of Communication like Oral Communication, Speech, Telephoning v/s. Face to Face Conversation, Active Listening, Interviews, Meetings and Written Communication includes Business Letter Writing, Memo and Report Writing.

The book provides numerous exercises; case studies, critical thinking and self-check questions, which will help to improve one's communication level and have great practical application in real life.

—Author

Acknowledgement

I would like to express my gratitude to all the people those who helped me in bringing out this book. I would like to express my thanks to my mother for her blessings and inspiration. This book is not only the desire of the author but also has been sharpened with the blessing and support of senior fellows.

I forward my sincere thanks to the renowned academicians Dr. Tarekegn Tedesse, President, Dr. Nulelegn Tefera, V/P Academics, Dr. Habtamu Hailu, V/P Research, Dr. Kurkura Katebo, V/P Administration, Dr. Zeleke Ewentu, V/P International Relations, Dr. Haftamu Itefa, Director, Academic Program Office, Addis Ababa Science & Technology University, Ethiopia.

I would like to thanks Mr. Teshome Abera, (Director), Mr. Abiyu Yenealem, Mr. Yemane Mehare from Corporate Communication Directorate, AASTU for their continuous support.

I extend my sincere thank to Dr. D .P. Sharma, Professor MAISM, Jaipur, Dr. Harsh Purohit, Dean, Wisdom, Faculty of Management Studies, Banasthali University, Dr. T.K. Jain, Dean, International School of Business Management, Jaipur, Dr. Srinivas Inguva, Professor, George Brown College, Toronto, Canada, Dr. Dinesh Sharma, Professor, Maryland University, USA, Dr. Kamal Nayan Agarwal, Associate Professor, Howard University, USA, Dr. Vinay Nangia, Professor, IIT Roorkee, Dr. R.K. Jaitley, Professor, Sharda University, Noida, Dr. Dewedi, Dean Research, SGV University, Jaipur, Dr. P.K. Gupta, Professor, Institute of Management Studies, Indore, Dr. Ibohal Meitei, Professor, Department of Management, Manipur University, Dr. R. K. Verma, Professor, Arba Minch University, Ethiopia, Dr. Himanshu Sharma, Nizwa College of Technology, Oman.

I also express my sincere gratitude to Dr. Duggasa Mulugeta, Dean, School of Business & Management, AASTU, Mr. Mengesha Yayo, HoD, Dr. Alula Asfaw, Mr. Andualem Deba, Mr. Elias, Mr. Gamechu Nemera, Mr. Mabratu Alemu, Mr. Amare Abawa, Management Department, and all my colleagues and friends for their inspiration.

I would like to acknowledge my wife Dr. Tripti Sharma, my sons Anubhav and Vaibhav, for having passions and extending moral support during working on this book.

At the end, I would like to express my sincere thanks to the publishers for showing their faith and confidence in bringing the book in present and nice form.

—Author

Contents

Part II: Media of Communication

Part I

AN OVERVIEW

1. Communication: An Overview
2. The Communication Process
3. Communication Principles
4. Types of Communication in Organization
5. Public Relations
6. Impact of Technological Advancement on Business Communication

CHAPTER 1

Communication
An Overview

Contents of the Chapter

- Meaning and Definition of Communication
- Significance of Communication
- Role of Communication in Management
- Importance of Communication

Learning Objectives

After finishing this chapter, students should be able to:

- Understand the meaning and definition of communication
- Explain the objectives of communication
- Know the role of communication in management
- Evaluate the importance of the communication

1.1 INTRODUCTION

Effective communication plays a vital role for every individual, groups and organizations to perform their day-to-day activity. The communication is an integral part human civilization. Communication is closely related with the human relations movement. No human relationship can be maintained in the absence of communication. Same in the case of organizations, no activity or coordination can be performed without communication. Communication is the main integrating constituent of any business. It is impossible for any business to nurture and inflate without proper communication among employees and other external associates of the Organizations. Communication is the base for everything we do, our success and failure totally depends on the effectiveness of communication. In an organization, the achievement or failure of the organizational goals, depends on the effective communication skills of its employees.

'Business Communication' is communication that takes place in an organizational context in order to exchange information, ideas, plans, and strategies, to offer the best of customer services and to make decisions, rules and regulations, proposals, contracts, and agreements, etc.

Communication is regarded as the "lifeblood" of every organization. We cannot think the existence of an organization without communication because it provides the information and that information becomes the basis of quality decision-making. Communication is crucial particularly to those who deal with people, work with and getting things done by people. Managers use communication to perform three basic functions:

- To gather and communicate information,
- To make decision and
- To endorse interpersonal relationship.

Managers are expected to work together with people to achieve organizational goals. All of these jobs happen through communication. Effective managers are able to use a wide variety of media & strategies to communicate. The success of any organization depends on the ability of its employees and managers to communicate effectively. Through effective communication, organizations increase productivity, anticipate problems, make decisions, coordinate workflow, develop relationships and promote products and services. In general, communication enables organizations to function.

1.2 MEANING AND DEFINITION OF COMMUNICATION

The word 'communication' has been derived from the Latin noun 'communis' and which means 'to share commonly'. Communication in its simplest sense involves two or more persons who come together to share, to dialogue or just to be together for a festival or family gathering. Talking with someone, arguing in a discussion, speaking in public, reading a newspaper, watching TV etc. are all different kinds of communication that we are engaged in everyday. Therefore, *Communication is a process of sharing or exchange of ideas, information, knowledge, attitude or feeling among two or more persons through certain signs and symbols.*

Definitions: Communication has been defined by different scholars and researchers in deferent point of time in different ways. Some of the definition includes:

- According to Hamilton and Parker (1987), communication is *"the process of people sharing thoughts, ideas, and feelings with each other in commonly understandable ways."*
- According to I.A. Richards defines *"Communication is the exchange of meanings between individuals through a common system of symbols."*
- According to Bovee and Thill (2000) communication is *"the process of sending and receiving messages"*. They distinguished communication and effective communication. According to Bovee and Thill, effective communication occurs when individual achieve a shared understanding, stimulate others to take actions, and encourage people to think in new ways.

- According to Wilbur Schramm "*communication is the mechanism through which human relations exist and develop.*"

1.3 SIGNIFICANCE OF COMMUNICATION

An organization is a group of people allied for business, political, professional, religious, athletic, social, or other reason. Its activities require human beings to interact, react and to communicate. They exchange information, ideas, plans, make decisions, rules, proposals, contracts and various agreements that cannot happen without communication.

Communication works as glue in the sharing of information among the parts of an organization, as well as between the organization and the outside world, that binds the organization together. As a member of an organization, be it formal or informal organization, we are a link in the communication chain. Communication skills are important because it is through communication that you gain the information you need to make successful decisions at work.

Researches indicate that communication skills were rated "extremely important" relative to other kinds of abilities by the surveyed organization. Researches conducted on business organizations also show that "inability to communicate" and "poor communication skills" were the most frequently mentioned reasons for not hiring a job applicant.

1.4 ROLE OF COMMUNICATION IN MANAGEMENT

Communication plays a very important role in an organization. Departments communicate from time to time in respect to daily activities and the organization's relationship with the external world.

The basic functions of the management can not be performed without communication. Planning, organizing, coordinating, budgeting, monitoring, controlling, staffing, delegation; and including marketing, production, financing, staffing (human resource managing), research and development, purchasing, selling, and so on could not be well coordinated, harnessed and their goals achieved without communication.

Communication plays a key role in meetings, any kind of senior.

The specific roles that communication plays include:

- Communication develops an understanding among the employees workers of the organization, which enhances the group efforts.
- Enhancing an attitude which is necessary for motivation, cooperation and job satisfaction.
- Communication discourages the spread of misinformation, ambiguity, rumors, which may be distractive for organizational performance.
- Communication encourages subordinates to provide suggestions for improving work environment.
- Communication helps in improving managements labor relations by keeping the communication channel open and accessible.
- Communication encourages social relations among workers by intercommunication.

1.5 IMPORTANCE OF COMMUNICATION

Communication will keep employees well-informed and give a business a higher productivity rate. Employees tend to have higher levels of job performance when there is a similarity of individual needs and job characteristics that exist and are communicated well. Sequentially, a happy and hard working team of employees helps give a business a corporate image that the public will find remarkable and attractive.

Importance of communication can be listed as under:

An aid to managerial performance. As management is a task of getting the work accomplished through efforts of other personnel, it is communication that can keep people working in harmony with desires of managers. Management members deal with work personnel in giving orders and instructions, in allocating jobs and duties, in approving work and recognizing performance, in explaining objectives and policies, and in seeking their effective co-operation. In all positive and negative actions, managers have to move with the help of communication in their dealings with human beings. Accordingly, the efficiency of a manager lies in his ability to communicate with other personnel.

Achieving coordination through understanding. Good communication stimulates human beings to put efforts in their work performance. The importance of the work is required to be mentally accepted before the doing of such work. That is, the will-to-do must precede the actual doing. To provide this will-to-do, communication creates an understanding and acceptance on the part of employees. As there can be no faith in an activity without understanding it clearly, communication results in satisfactory performance through creating this faith. In short, effective communication increases understanding of employees, gains their willing acceptance and leads them to greater efforts.

Helps in decision-making. Good communication system provides all necessary information, which enables a manager to take quality decision in the proper time and these decisions are communicated to those who are in need of them.

Base for leadership action. Leadership action is impossible without communication between the leader and his followers. The leader can exert his influence only through conveying ideas, feelings, suggestions and decisions to his followers. The followers too can convey their responses, feelings, attitudes and problems to the leader through the medium of communication. The two-way personal communication is essential for maintaining man-to-man relationship in leadership. Accordingly, effectiveness of leadership is greatly determined by the adequacy and clarity of communication.

Means of coordination. Communication helps in securing desired coordination of enterprise operations by communication network throughout the organization. As teamwork is essential for the accomplishment of jobs in many cases, coordination appears to be of paramount importance. For the purpose of coordination, managers keep the group fully informed of all facts and situations relating to the work. Secrecy creates suspicion and separates people; common understanding of common problems unites them for showing a better record of their performance.

Provision of job satisfaction. Mutual trust and confidence between management and workers can be increased by the communication of what the manager wants and what the employees perform. A clear-cut understanding provides job satisfaction to the employees, creates their confidence in the ability of managers and promotes their loyalty towards the enterprise. That is to say, effective communication satisfies personal and social needs of human beings and stimulates their job interest and enthusiasm.

Case Stuty: Across Cultures

A Chinese plane crashed a few years ago, when it tried to land in the fog but didn't pull up in time. The plane had a ground proximity warning system in English, which blared "pull up, pull up." The Chinese pilot"s last words on the cockpit recorder were,

"What does 'pull up' mean?"

In the air, a plane is its own world—with its own rules and communication needs. Flight attendants on international flights must be able to understand their passengers, and vice versa, for both service and safety's sake. The captain needs to be able to communicate with everyone, including control tower around the world.

A specific problem for aircraft maintenance personnel is that most carriers no longer translate their technical manuals into the local language because it is very costly, is a slow process, is prone to error, and leaves the carrier legally liable for any translation errors.

Airline technical manuals are now prepared in English only.

A specific type of English, called Simplified English, has been developed to meet the needs of airlines. Simplified English consists of simplified vocabulary and a simplified set of writing rules for using that vocabulary. The use of Simplified English is now required for the documentation of all civilian aircraft worldwide.

Simple English vocabulary was derived by a word count of samples of maintenance documentation. It contains a dictionary of approved words (approximately 1,000) and a set of writing rules.

Sentences cannot be longer than 20 words, and every paragraph must begin with a topic sentence and can contain no more than six sentences. Semicolons are not allowed, and in procedures, only the active voice is permitted.

The purpose of Simplified English and increased English training for all airline personnel is to improve both service and safety to the flying public.

Source: Scot Ober, Contemporary Business Communication, 7e Boston: Houghton Miffl in Company, 2009.

Critical Thinking

How well do you think Simplified English would work in typical written business communication? Why?

Summary

- Communication is the process of people sharing thoughts, ideas, and feelings with each other in commonly understandable ways.
- No human relationship can be maintained in the absence of communication. Same in the case of organizations no activity or coordination can be performed without communication.
- Communication is a process of sharing or exchanging of ideas, information, knowledge, attitude or feeling among two or more persons through certain signs and symbols.
- "Business Communication" is communication that takes place in an organizational context in order to exchange information, ideas, plans, and strategies, to offer the best of customer services and to make decisions, rules and regulations, proposals, contracts, and agreements, etc.
- Communication has plenty of advantages to organizations and group satisfaction, smooth management, labor relationship, and discourage the rumors, etc.
- Communication helps managers to enhance their performance, achieving coordinations, in decision making, leadership actions and for job satisfaction.

Exercises

1. How do you define communication?
2. Explain business communication.
3. Explain the significance
4. What is the role of communication in management of business?
5. How communication is important to them mangers of any organization?

Self-Check Questions

1. The Effective communication occurs when:
   (A) Individuals achieve the shared understanding.
   (B) Stimulate others to take action.
   (C) Encourages others to think in a new ways
   (D) A & B Only
   (E) All of above
2. Identify the wrong statement regarding the specific roles of communication:
   (A) Develops information & understanding.
   (B) Enhances the attitude necessary for job satisfaction.
   (C) Improve & upgrades the management- labor relations.
   (D) Encourages the rumors or misunderstandings.
   (E) None of the above
3. Identify the wrong statement regarding the significance of communication:
   (A) Provides information necessary to make successful decision at work.
   (B) The success of organization depends on the communication skills of its employee.
   (C) Communication skill is rated extremely important relative to other kinds of abilities.
   (D) None of above
   (E) All of the above

Answers

1. E 2. D 3. D

CHAPTER 2

The Communication Process

Contents of the Chapter

- Elements of the Communication Process
- The Process of Communication
- Barriers to Communication
- Guidelines to Overcome Communication Problem

Learning Objectives

After finishing this chapter, students should be able to:

- Understand the elements involved in a communication process
- Explain the communication process
- Know the barriers of effective communication
- Understand the methods to overcome from barriers of communication

2.1 INTRODUCTION

Communication is an active process which involves a series of actions and reactions with a view to achieving a goal. Communication, is a complex process undertaken to have a shared importance among the sender and receiver, this also has many elements involved in the communication model. The communication mix intermingle together several different elements. Many of the problems that occur in an organization are the direct result of people failing to communicate. Faulty communication causes the most problems. It leads to confusion and can cause a good plan to fail. Communication is the exchange and flow of information and ideas from one person to another. It involves a sender transmitting an idea to a receiver. And effective communication occurs only if the receiver understands the exact information or idea that the sender intends to transmit.

2.2 ELEMENTS OF THE COMMUNICATION PROCESS

The various elements of communication are briefly described here to understand the process of communication.

The process of communication involves five elements:

- Sender-Encoder
- Message
- Medium
- Receiver-Decoder
- Feedback

2.2.1 Sender/Encoder

The sender or the encoder *is the person who transmits, initiates, spreads, or communicates a message* or operates an electronic device with the purpose of informing, persuading, influencing, and changing the attitude, opinion, or behavior of the receiver (audience listener). He/she decides the communication symbols, the channel, and the time for sending the message after carefully considering the total situation in which communication takes place.

Ideas or Thoughts

Ideas or thoughts are the raw form of telling the ideas that the sender wants to share with a receiver by changing them to messages using symbols.

Encoding: *It is the changing of the raw idea from its mental form into symbols, that is, patterns of words, gestures, pictorial forms or signs (physical or sounds) of a specific visual /oral language. The sender must choose certain words or non-verbal methods to send an intentional message. This activity is called encoding.*

2.2.2 Message

Messages *are the signals and symbols used to convey the meaning.* It is the information, written, verbal or non-verbal, which is to be sent from one person to another. A great deal of skill and effort is required to formulate a message, the meaning of which should be understandable to the receiver. A message can enhance or distort effective communication. For instance, in an interview your intention is to impress interviewer, but if you give answers whose meaning is not clear, the interviewer may perceive that you are incompetent for the job.

Whenever we compose a message, we need to consider what content to include, how the receiver will interpret it, and how it may affect your relationship. The form of message whether verbal or non-verbal depends upon the purpose of the communication. It is necessary that the message sent by the communicator is clear and precise.

2.2.3 Medium

Medium is the carrier of the message such as written words, in the form of written communication, and spoken words and gestures in the form of face-to-face discussion.

Channel

A channel is a vehicle through which a message is carried from the communicator to the receiver. For instance, a memo or a letter, which carry the written words, and air, radio, telephone, television and so on etc that carry the spoken words.

The success or failure of a communication depend on the selection of the right channel. Actually the intention would be to reach out to the maximum number of people but for efficient communication attempt should be to minimize time and cost in the total information exchange effort.

2.2.4 Receiver/Decoder

Receiver is the targeted audience of the message. A receiver is any person who notices and attaches some meaning to a message.

Decoding

Decoding is the act of translating symbols of communication into their ordinary meanings; however, the total meaning would consist of meanings of the words (symbols) together with the tone and the attitude of the sender as treated by the structure of the message and the choice of words used by him (the sender).

2.2.5 Feedback

Feedback is the response or acknowledgement of receiver to the communicator's message. This provides the communicator an opportunity to improve and make his communication effective. This is the loop that connects the receiver in the communication process with the sender, who, in turn, acts as a feedback receiver and, thus, gets to know that communication has been accomplished. In communication, feedback plays an important role. It helps the communicator know if there are any corrections or changes to be made in the proposed action. It also ensures that the receiver has received the message and understood it as intended by the sender. Feedback, thus, provides an opportunity to evaluate what is right or wrong about a particular communication. It helps to regulate the conversation among two or more individuals and also stimulates and strengthens an idea that is desired to be communicated.

2.3 THE PROCESS OF COMMUNICATION

Communication is a process that involves certain distinct steps. In its simpler form, it relates to stimulus and response. The stimulus arises from the communicator, and the receiver responds. Communication is not complete till the message conveyed by the sender is properly understood by the receiver. Communication involves participants (a sender and a receiver), message to be sent, a medium to carry the communication signals and the environments in which the message is sent and received. These elements act and interact in the five-step process. Whether you are speaking or writing, listening or reading, communication is more than a single act. Instead, it is a chain of events that can be broken into five phases as:

- The sender has an idea
- The idea becomes a message
- The message is transmitted
- The receiver gets the message
- The receiver reacts and sends feedback to the sender

2.3.1 The Sender Has an Idea

The sender is the individual who initiates the communication. This person is sometimes known as the "encoder", two things must happen before the sender wants to send a message which are as follows.

First, an internal or external stimulus prompts sender to send a message. This prompt may arrive in the form of letters, memorandum, penciled note, electronic mail, fax, telex, or even casual conversation in the hallway. Regardless of the stimulus source; it could be a business transaction, a written question, a meeting, an interview, or unexpected request for a favour. Whatever the case might be, sender will start thinking of ideas for the message.

The second requirement to send message is sufficient motivation. Think of times when a manager asks a question, and some of the people present were fairly sure they knew the answer (were stimulated), but did not respond. Why didn't they respond? Probably, because they were not sufficiently motivated, i.e. they saw no personal benefit in answering. Or they saw greater benefit in not answering.

2.3.2 The Idea Becomes a Message

After being stimulated and motivated to communicate, the sender must decide how best to convey a message to the specific receiver. The message is the information or core idea being transmitted. The process of putting a message into the form in which it is to be communicated is called **encoding**. It consists of both verbal (written or spoken) symbols and nonverbal (unspoken) symbols. Verbal information is the part of the message that is read heard. Nonverbal information entails such things as body language and the surrounding environment. Whenever we compose a message, we need to consider what content to include, how the receiver will interpret it, and how it may affect your relationship.

"A simple 'Thank you' message will be relatively easy. In contrast, to inform 200 employees of bad news about salaries will require much more complicated, carefully planned message."

To some extent, the choice of words also depends on our cultural background. The nature of our code—our language and vocabulary—imposes its own limits on our message. For example, the language of a lawyer differs from that of an accountant or a doctor, and the difference in their vocabularies affects their ability to recognize and express ideas.

Challenges of Formulating Messages

Several things can go wrong when we are formulating a message. Typical problems involved are indecision about message content, lack of familiarity with the situation or the receiver, emotional conflicts, or difficulty in expressing ideas.

1. **Indecision about content:** Deciding what to say is the first difficulty in the communication process. Many people make the mistake of trying to convey everything they know about a subject. When a message contains too much information, it is difficult to absorb. If you want to get your point across, therefore, you have to decide what to include and what to leave out, how much detail to provide, and what order to include and what order adequate background. Include only the information that is useful to the receiver, and organize it in a way that encourages its acceptance.
2. **Lack of familiarity with the situation or the receiver:** Can we deliver our message equally well when we are not very familiar with the subject we are talking about: or when we do not know the receiver very well? Creating an effective message is difficult if we don't know how it will be used. Let's say we are writing a report on the market for sports equipment. If we don't know the purpose of the report, it's hard to know what to say. Some of the things you should be clear about before writing the report are:
   - What sort of sports equipment should be covered?
   - Should you include team sports as well as individual sports?
   - Should you subdivide the market geographically or according to price ranges?
   - How long should the report be?

Unless we know why the report is needed, we really cannot answer these questions intelligently. We are forced to create a very general document one that covers a little bit of everything.

Lack of familiarity with our audience is an equally serious handicap we need to know something about the biases, education, age, status, and style of the receiver in order to create an effective message. If we are writing for a specialist in our field, for example, we can use technical terms that might be unfamiliar to a layperson. If we are addressing a lower-level employee, we might approach a subject differently than if we were talking to our boss. Decisions about the content, organization, style, and tone of your message all depend, at least to some extent, on the relationship between us and our audience. If we don't know the audience, we will be forced to make these decisions in the dark. As a result, at least part of our message may miss the point. Hence, ask why we are preparing the message and for whom we are preparing it.

3. **Emotional conflicts:** Another potential problem in developing the message arises when the sender has conflicting emotions about the subject or the audience. Let's say we've been asked to recommend ways to improve the organization of our department. We conclude that the best approach is to combine two positions. But this solution will mean eliminating the job of one of our close associates. As we prepare our report, we find ourselves apologizing for our recommendation. Even though we believe our position is justified, we cannot make a convincing case. Thus, in business communications try to maintain your objectivity.
4. **Difficulty of expressing ideas:** Most of us might think that to write and to speak are not so difficult. We only learn that they do not come easy when we have to make public speeches or when we are a required to write an influential letter on a particular matter. Lack of experience in writing or speaking can also prevent a person from developing effective messages. Some people have limited education or a lack of aptitude when it comes

to expressing ideas. Perhaps they have a limited vocabulary or are uncertain about questions of grammar, punctuation, and style. Or perhaps they are simply frightened by the idea of writing something or appearing before as they lack expertise in using language.

Problems of this sort can be overcomed, but only with some effort. The important thing is to recognize the problem and take action. An inability to put thoughts into words can be overcomed through study and practice.

2.3.3 The Message is Transmitted

The third step in the communication process is physical transmission of the message from sender to receiver. How will we send our message? Should one write or speak? What is the appropriate channel for any given message? The channel is the means used to convey the message. The forms of communication may be verbal, or non verbal. Beyond that, we can convey a message by phone, computer, face-to-face exchange, or other medium.

2.3.4 The Receiver Gets the Message

The receiver is the individual to whom the message is directed, also known as the *decoder*. When the encoder's message is picked up, the receiver tries to make sense out of it, i.e. to decode it. Decoding is the process the receiver goes through in trying to interpret the exact meaning of the message. Everyone tries to read between the lines in an effort to interpret what the sender means by the message. If we send a letter, the recipient has to read it before she/he can understand it. If we are giving a speech, the people in the audience have to be able to hear us, and they have to be paying attention.

But physical reception is only the first step. The receiver also has to absorb the message mentally. In other words, the message has to be understood and stored in the receiver's mind. If all goes well, the message is interpreted correctly. The receiver assigns the same basic meaning to the words as the sender intended and responds in the desired way.

Like transmission problems, problems during the reception phase often have a physical cause. Competing sights and sounds, an uncomfortable chair, poor lighting or some other irritating condition may distract the receiver. In some impairment, for example, or even a headache, can interfere with reception of a message. These annoyances do not generally block communication entirely, but they may reduce the receiver's concentration.

Perhaps the most common barrier to reception is simply lack of attention on the receiver's part. We all let our minds wander now and then, regardless of how hard we try to concentrate. People are especially likely to drift off when they are forced to listen to information that is difficult to understand or that has little direct bearing on their own lives. If they are tired or concerned about other matters, they are even more likely to lose interest.

2.3.5 The Receiver Reacts and Sends Feedback to the Sender

Feedback is the receiver's response to a message. It is the final link in the communication chain. However, the feedback response involves a reversal of the communication process so that the receiver now becomes the sender and the sender becomes the receiver. After getting the message, the receiver responds in some way and signals as a response to the sender. The signal may take the form of a smile, a long pause, a spoken comment, a written message, or an action. Even a lack of response is, in a sense, a form of response.

Feedback is a key element in the communication process because it enables the sender to evaluate the effectiveness of the message. It provides guidance for the next message that you send to the receiver. If your audience doesn't understand what you mean, you can tell by the response and refine the message. Feedback plays an important role by indicating significant communication barriers: differences in background, different interpretations of words, and differing emotional reactions. So when the receiver of the message has made feedback and the sender is sure that the message has been communicated in the way intended, we say communication has existed.

Therefore, from the above phases, you can think of communication as a process consisting of identifiable links, with ultimate objective of influencing behavior, attitudes, and beliefs. Each element of the communication process is critical: the sender, encoding, channel, the receiver, decoding, and feedback.

The communication process has been illustrated in the figure given below:

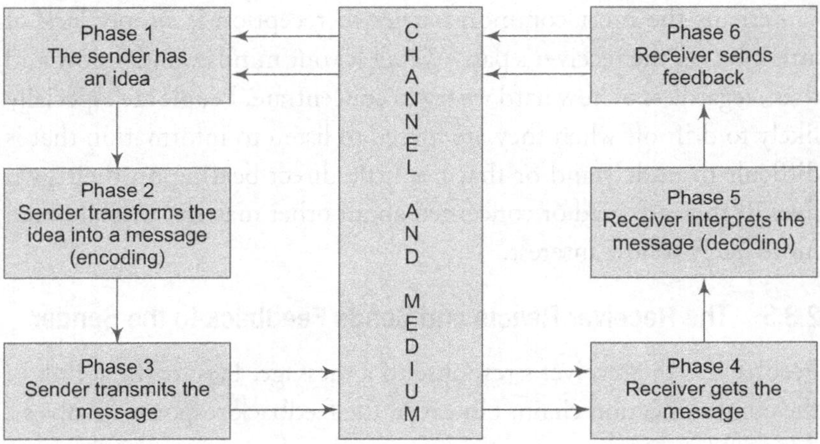

2.4 BARRIERS OF EFFECTIVE COMMUNICATION

Communication is successful only when the receiver understands the message as intended by the sender. *Organizational communication* is the process by which managers develop a system to give information and transmit meaning to large number of people within the organization and to relevant individuals and institutions outside it. Communication is very important because:

- Managers spend most of their time communicating
- Communication is needed for managerial effectiveness
- Communication leads to power
- Communication leads to organizational effectiveness

But many a time managers say something and the subordinates understand it differently. This distortion may be due to some barriers to communication, which are discussed as follows.

2.4.1 Communication Barriers Between People

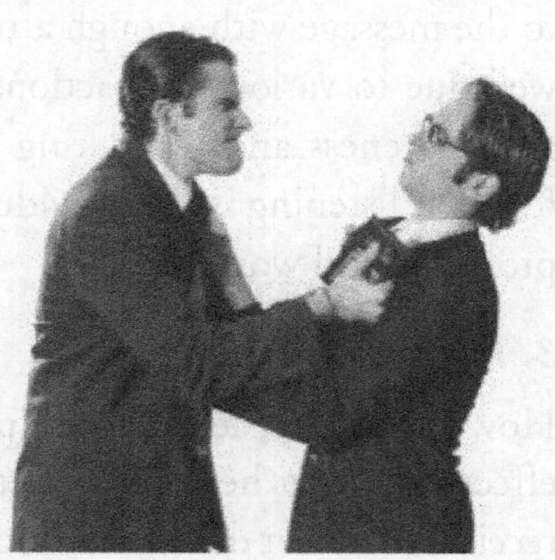

These include barriers such as differences in perception and language, poor listening, emotional interference, cultural differences and physical distractions.

1. Differences in Perception and Language

Perception is people's individual interpretation of the sensory world around them. Even when two people have experienced the same event, their mental images of that event will not be identical. Because perceptions are unique, the ideas one want to express differ from other people.

Language is an arbitrary code that depends on shared definitions. A receiver and a sender may attach different meanings to the words used in a message. The receiver will interpret the message based on his experiences, interests, opinions and emotions. Communicated message must be understandable to the receiver. Words mean different things to different people. Language reflects not only the personality of the individual but also the culture of society in which the individual is living. In organizations, people come from different regions, different backgrounds, speak different languages, have different academic backgrounds, different intellectual facilities, and hence the terminology they use varies. Often, communication gaps arise because the language the sender is using may be incomprehensible, vague and indigestible.

2. Poor Listening

Poor listening is one of the major communication problems. Listening ability decreases when information is difficult to understand and when it has little meaning for the listener. Failure to listen is a common barrier to successful oral communication. Most people speak 100 to 200 words a minute but are capable of listening to material of average difficulty at 500 or more words a minute. This difference allows listener's mind to wander to topics other than the message. Listening is a skill that can and must be learned.

Misunderstanding and conflicts can be reduced if people would listen to the message with enough attention. Most people do not listen very well due to various distractions, emotions, excitement, indifference, aggressiveness and wandering attention. One of the major reasons for poor listening is an individual's continual thinking about his own problems and worries.

3. Emotional Interference

How the receiver feels at the time of receipt of information influences effectively how he interprets the information. For example, if the receiver feels that the communicator is in a cheerful mood, he interprets that information being sent by the communicator to be good and interesting. Extreme emotions and joyousness or depression are quite likely to hinder the effectiveness of communication. It is difficult to shape a message when one is upset, hostile or fearful. The ideas and feelings often get in the way of being objective.

4. Cultural Differences

Communicating with someone from another country is probably the most extreme example of how different backgrounds and cultures may impede communication. In fact, it may be one of the hardest communication barriers to overcome.

5. Receiver's Capability

If the receiver has a physical or mental disability that causes a communication barrier, the sender should recognize this in choosing message type and channel.

6. Physical Distractions

Communication barriers are often physical: bad connections, poor acoustics, or illegible copy. This can block an effective message. The receiver might be distracted by poor lighting, health problems or some other irritating condition, that may reduce the receiver's concentration.

2.4.2 Communication Barriers within Organizations

The number of business messages delivered each day is staggering, and the opportunities for feedback are often limited, making it difficult to correct misunderstandings when they do occur.

1. Information Overloads and Message Competition

A recent study by the Gallup organization found that, the average white-collar worker sends and receives as many as 190 messages a day. The problem is that new technology is not replacing more traditional forms; it is just adding to the load.

2. Environmental Factors

The environment in which communication occurs can interfere with the success of a message. One such example of a distracting environmental factor is a noisy machine in an area where a supervisor is trying to speak with an employee.

3. Incorrect Filtering

Filtering is screening out information before a message is passed on to someone. Information theory tells us "every relay doubles the noise and cuts the message in half". That means the message will be distilled and probably distorted before it is passed on to the intended receiver.

4. Closed or Inadequate Communication Channel

A management style that is directive and authoritative blocks the free and open exchange of information that characterizes effective communication. Having too few channels will block communication, whereas having too many channels will distort messages as they move upward, downward or horizontally through the organization.

2.4.3 Channel Selection

Communication may be oral, written, visual or audio-visual. The different communication channels can be personal barriers in that some individuals always seem to incline toward a particular channel even though a more effective one exists. All the media have their relative merits and limitations. While a properly chosen medium can add to the effectiveness of a communication, an unsuitable medium may act as a barrier to it.

Appropriate Uses of Communication Media	
Medium	**When to use the Message**
E-Mail	• Consists of short, simple content. • Involves mostly fact-based information where visual and nonverbal cues are not required. • Requires, prompt dissemination or response.
Face-to-Face	• Will benefit from visual, verbal, and non-verbal cues. • Requires exploration of complex topics. • Involves sensitive, personal, or bad-news information. • Requires interactive or immediate feedback.
Telephone	• Will benefit from set less-formal environment. • Requires an audience of one (usually). • Requires discussion with immediate feedback off common ideas.
Written	• Requires at record for documentation ox later reference. • Contains complex, detailed, or lengthy content. • Benefits from, graphics or other visuals.

Source: Scot Ober, *Contemporary Business Communication*, 7e Boston: Houghton Mifflin Company, 2009

2.4.4 Physical Barriers

These include noise, time and distance.

1. Noise

Noise is an interruption that can creep in at any point of the communication process and make it ineffective. Environment is one major cause that interferes with message reception like noises from the roadside, by the loud noise of machines in factories, constant gossiping of individuals outside the communication act, blaring loudspeaker, faulty transmission, and so on. Noise can occur in other forms also; poor handwriting, heavy accent or soft speech, communication in a poorly lit room, and so on, in fact, these are barriers to effective communication.

For smooth and effective communication, it is necessary to eliminate or reduce noise as far as possible.

2. Time

The frequency of communication encounters affects the human relationships and the intensity of human relations is affected by the amount of time that passes between these encounters. If the employee does not communicate with their superiors for a long time, it may create a communication gap between them, which may affect their relationship.

Time can act as a barrier to communication in some other ways also. A guest who arrives at midnight will not be able to communicate well with the host who might feel embarrassed or disturbed in his sleep. Time will not allow two communicators to talk to each other if they work in different shifts. A phone call at midnight can irritate or embarrass the receiver.

3. Distance

The distance between the communicator and the receiver can be a strong barrier to communication, if the technical devices of communication such as telephone, telefax, internet are not available to link them. Even faulty sitting arrangement in the office can create a kind of communication gap, which can be eliminated by adjusting the distance.

2.4.5 Semantics

This refers to the different uses and meanings of words and symbols. Words and symbols may not have similar uses and meanings for different individuals from different cultural group, language and living style so it may create some barrier in the communication process. It is found by the experts that people attributes 14,000 different meanings to 500 commonly used English words. Therefore, the sender and receiver are many a time likely to attribute different meaning to the same word. Sometimes, they may use different words to communicate the same meaning. There are many words in English such as light, cheap, end so on.

Semantic Barriers Include

1. **Interpretations of words:** Receivers decode words and phrases in conformity with their own network, which may be very different from those of senders. Words are capable of communicating a variety of meanings. It is quite possible that the receiver do not assign the same meaning to a word as the sender has intended, that may lead to miscommunication. For some, a successful career means having prestigious job title and making lot of money; for others, it may mean having a job they really enjoy and plenty of personal time to spend with family and friends.
2. **Bypassed instructions:** When the message sender and receiver attribute different meanings to the same words, bypassing often occurs.

Example: An office manager handed to a new assistant a letter, with the instruction "Take it to our store room and burn it". In the office manager's mind (and in the firm's jargon) the word "burn" meant to make a copy on a photocopier. As the letter was extremely important, she wanted an extra copy. However, the confused employee afraid to ask questions burnt the letter and thus destroyed the original existing copy!

To avoid communication errors of bypassing, when you give instructions or discuss issues, be sure your words and sentences will convey the intended meaning to the recipient. Also, when you are the recipient of unclear instruction, before acting on it, ask questions to determine the sender intended meaning.

3. **Denotations, Connotations, and Euphoniums.**

   Denotations: The denotative meaning is the meaning on which most people will probably agree. A denotation is usually the dictionary definition of a word. Denotative meanings name objects, people or events without indicating positive or negative qualities. Such words as car, desk, book, house, and water convey denotative meanings. The receiver has a similar understanding of the thing in which the word is used.

Connotations: In addition to more literal denotative meanings, some words have connotative meanings that arouse qualitative judgments and personal reactions. The term 'meeting room' is denotative. The word man is denotative, father, prophet, brother are connotative. Some words have positive connotations in some contexts and negative meanings in others. For example, slim girl and slim chances.

Euphemisms: Tactful writer and speakers use euphemisms whenever possible to replace words that might have blunt, painful, lowly or distasteful connotations. Euphemisms are mild, innovative expressions with which most people do not have negative associations.

2.4.6 Perception of Reality

Francis Bacon has said, *'Man prefers to believe what he prefers to be true'*. The individual experiences and their interpretations are never identical because their perceptions are different. If two friends see a movie together, their interpretation, of the events and the characters in it will certainly be different.

The reality of an object, an event, or a person is different to different people. Reality is not a fixed concept; it is complex, infinite and continually changing. Besides, each human being has limited sensory perceptions—touch, sight, hearings, smell, and taste and each person's mental filter is unique. People perceive reality in different ways. No two persons perceive reality in identical manners.

2.4.7 Attitudes and Opinions

Communication effectiveness is influenced also by the attitudes and opinions the communicators have in their mental filters. People tend to react favourably when the message they receive agrees with their views towards the information, the set of facts, and the sender. In addition, sometimes unrelated circumstances affect their attitudes, and responses as follows.

- Emotional state
- Favourable or Unfavourable information
- Closed mind
- Status consciousness
- Credibility

2.4.8 Information Overload

It refers to the condition of having too much information to process. The implication is that individuals can effectively process only certain amount of information. An example would be if your professor gave you too much information, too quickly, concerning a term paper's requirements or if a manager gave an employee too much information at one time about a report's requirements. In either situation, the receiver probably does not receive the entire message. Managers need to be aware of potential for information overload and to make appropriate adjustments.

2.5 GUIDELINES TO OVERCOME COMMUNICATION BARRIERS

To make communication effective, managers must attempt to remove barriers. There are six factors or themes that contribute to effective communication.

1. Fostering an open communication climate
2. Committing to ethical communication
3. Understanding the difficulties involved in intercultural communication
4. Adopting an audience-centered approach to communication
5. Using technology wisely and responsibly to obtain and share information
6. Creating and processing messages effectively and efficiently

1. Fostering an open communication climate: An organization's communication climate is a reflection of its corporate culture: the mixture of values, traditions and habits. It affects the quantity and quality of the information that passes through the pipeline.

(a) *Modify the number of organizational levels:* One way to foster an open communication climate is to reduce the number of levels in the organizations structure. The fewer the links in the communication chain, the less likely the misunderstandings will occur. In other words, a flat structure (having fewer levels) and a wide span of control are likely to introduce distortion than a tall structure and a narrow span of control.

(b) *Facilitate feedback:* Giving the audience a chance to provide feedback is crucial to maintaining an open communication climate.

2. Committing to ethical communication: Ethics are the principles of conduct that govern a person or a group. Ethical people are generally trustworthy, fair and impartial, respecting the rights of others, and concerned about the impact of their actions on society. Ethics plays of a crucial role in communication. Ethical communication includes all relevant information, which is true in every sense and is not deceptive in any way.

(a) *Recognize ethical choices:* Every company has responsibilities to various groups—customers, shareholders, suppliers, neighbors, the community and the nation. What is right for one group may be wrong for another. Moreover as we attempt to satisfy the needs of one group, we may be presented with an option that seems right on the surface but somehow feels wrong.

(b) *Make ethical choices:* Laws provide ethical guidelines for certain types of messages. Look at the consequences of the decision and opt for the solution that provides the greatest good to the greatest number of people, and one that we can live with.

(c) *Motivate ethical choices:* Organizations can foster ethical behavior:

- by helping top managers become more sensitive communicators
- by using ethics audits
- by rewarding ethical actions

3. Understanding the difficulties involved in intercultural communication: More and more businesses are crossing national boundaries to compete on a global scale and the make up of the global and domestic work force is changing rapidly. Global companies must understand the laws, customs and business practices of many countries, and they must deal with business associates and employees.

4. Adopting an audience-centered approach to communication: Using an audience-centered approach means keeping the audience in mind all times when communicating. Since audience is taken care of, every possible step is taken to get the message across in a way that is meaningful to the audience. Empathizing with and being sensitive to the audience's feelings is the best way to overcome such communication barriers as differences in perception and emotional interference.

5. Using technology wisely and responsibly to obtain and share information: In today's world, information moves through an array of media at the speed of a neural impulse. Technology has such an impact on business communication. When used wisely and responsibly, technology helps to improve the effectiveness of business communication.

6. Creating and processing messages effectively and efficiently: The sixth guideline is to plan messages, generate ideas, organize the thoughts, and turn the words into effective business messages.

(a) *Learn about the audience:* Creating an effective message is difficult if the audience is unfamiliar, or if we don't know how the message will be used. We need to know something about the biases, education, age, status and style of the receiver in order to create an effective message.

(b) *Adapt the message to the audience:* Decisions about the content, organization, style, and tone of the message depend on the relationship between the sender and the audience.

(c) *Develop and connect ideas:* Include only the information that is useful to the audience, and organize it in such a way that encourages its acceptance. To make message memorable not the following.

- Use telling statistics
- Use words that evoke a physical, sensory impression
- Tie the message to the audience's frame of reference
- Keep messages as brief and as clean as possible
- Highlighting and summarizing key points

(d) *Reduce the number of messages:* Organizations save time and money by sending only necessary messages. If a written message merely adds to the information overload, it is probably better left unsent or handled some other way—by a quick telephone call or a face to face chat. By holding down the number of messages, organizations will maximize the benefits of their communication activities.

(e) *Choose the correct channel and medium:* The careful choice of channel and medium helps focus the audience's attention on message. The choice of a communication channel and medium depends on the:

- Message
- Audience
- Need for speed
- Situation.

(f) *Strengthen the communication skills:* Recognizing the importance of efficient communication, many companies today train employees in communication skills. Companies offer seminars and workshops on handling common oral communication situations (such as dealing with customers, managing subordinates, and getting along with co-workers), as well as training in computers and other electronic means of communication.

2.6 TEN COMMANDMENTS OF EFFECTIVE COMMUNICATION

1. Listen attentively, find areas of common interest, and listen for main ideas.
2. Plan ahead, be prepared, avoid important situations if possible, and keep the message brief.

3. Avoid stereotyping and assignment of individuals or ideas to right categories.
4. Distinguish between the desire to know and the need to know.
5. Distinguish among facts, references and conclusions.
6. Avoid attributing motives to others.
7. Attend to behavioral cues as well a language direction.
8. Say enough, but leave something unsaid.
9. Don't ignore all conflicts, but avoid the unnecessary conflict.
10. Withhold value judgments about context or delivery, until strategically appropriate.

2.7 EFFECTIVE LISTENING

Effective listening is important to communicate effectively. The following are the useful pointers in this direction.

- Stop talking
- Put the speaker at ease
- Demonstrate that you want to listen
- Remove distractions
- Empathize with the speaker
- Be patient
- Hold your temper
- Don't argue
- Ask question

Summary

- Communication is a process whereby various elements are participating in its model. The elements of communication includes the sender, (encoding process), the media, the message, the receiver (decoding process), and feedback.
- The sender is the initiator of the communication process, who encodes the message in a way that the receiver can understand it.

- The message is the information that the sender wants to communicate with the receiver of the message.
- The medium is the channel through which information can be directed to the receiver.
- The receiver is the targeted audience, who understands the message through the decoding process.
- Feedback is the necessary loop of the communication. Feedback helps sender to understand that the message is delivered as it is intended.
- Feedback provides an opportunity to evaluate what is right or wrong about a particular communication. It helps to regulate the conversation among two or more individuals and also stimulates and reinforces an idea that is desired to be communicated.
- Communication involves participants (a sender and a receiver), message to be sent through a medium to carry the communication and the environments in which the message is sent and received.
- There are barriers in the communication process from the way information is prepared by the sender to the information is understood by the receiver. These barriers may occur between the people, within the organization, channel selection and physical barriers.
- These problems are alleviated through curies preparation of the message by the sender considering the receiver, selecting appropriate media of communication, encouraging feedback and considering the physical appearance of the message.

Exercises

1. Discuss the elements of a communication process.
2. What is encoding and Decoding? Explain.
3. Explain the process of communication.
4. What are barriers to effective communication?
5. Discuss the role of feedback in communication.
6. Write down the communication barriers which lie among the people.
7. How communication barrier occurs within the organization?
8. Channel selection can be a barrier in the communication process. Explain it.
9. Explain point wise to overcome from the communication barrier.
10. What are the points to be considered to be an effective listener?

Self-Check Questions

1. An individual who initiates the communication is
   - A. Sender
   - B. Receiver
   - C. Decoder
   - D. Decoding
   - E. None of the above
2. The means used to convey the message
   - A. Channel
   - B. Decoding
   - C. Encoding
   - D. Message
   - E. All
3. The conditions of having too much information to process is called
   - A. Over using one channel
   - B. Perceptions of reality
   - C. Barriers of channel selection
   - D. Information overloads
   - E. None
4. In order to overcome from the problem of communication barriers, organization can;
   - A. Commit to the ethical communication
   - B. Adopt an audience centered approach
   - C. Use technology responsibly in obtaining and sharing information
   - D. B & C
   - E. All of above

Answers

1. A 2. A 3. D 4. E

Chapter 3

Communication Principles

Contents of the Chapter

- The 7 "C"s of Communication
- Completeness
- Conciseness
- Consideration
- Concreteness
- Clarity
- Courtesy
- Correctness

Learning Objectives

After finishing this chapter, students should be able to:

- Understand the 7 C's of communication
- Know about the completeness, conciseness, consideration and concreteness of communication
- Explain the role of clarity, courtesy and correctness in communication

3.1 INTRODUCTION

Building effective communication skills is essential for anyone whether we want to succeed in business or personal relationships. These communication skills, both—oral and written, are the foundation for helping you express yourself clearly and correctly. When there it poor communication in an organization, there can be any number of negative outcomes, including errors, productivity declines, distrust, lower morale, confusion, absenteeism, and general dissatisfaction. As a leader or manager, you are expected constantly to advise, inform, explain, discuss, review, counsel, guide, suggest, persuade, convince, coach, humor, and respond. Employees seek a leader or manager who is open, accessible, and responsive.

3.2 7 "C"S OF COMMUNICATION

Communication is an important part of our world today. The ability to communicate effectively with others is considered as a prized quality of the successful business people. To communicate and compose effective message, we need to follow certain scientific principles. As a leader or manager to make our letters, memorandums, reports, representations and any other form of communication we need to stick on these communication principles. They are also referred to as the 7 "C"s because all of them begin with the alphabet "C".

The 7 "C"s of communication are as follows:

- Completeness
- Conciseness
- Consideration
- Concreteness
- Clarity
- Courtesy
- Correctness

3.3 COMPLETENESS

A business communication has to be complete. In business communication completeness of all necessary fact is absolutely necessary. Message is "complete" when it contains all facts the reader or listener needs for the reaction descried. An incomplete message irritates the receiver. Due to incomplete messages there may be wrong actions, which may prove expensive to an organization.

We should prepare our messages in way that the receiver has no doubt about anything contained in it. *For instance*, you are ordering a shirt through mail, your mail must include all necessary facts such as color, size, quantity, mode of payment, and order date and so on without these details order may not be fulfilled as per your satisfaction.

There are several grounds necessary for the completeness of messages:

- Complete message are more likely to bring the desired results without the extra cost of additional messages.
- Complete messages serve in developing and building goodwill.
- Complete message develops a sense of concern for other party as both the reader and sender may have different background, culture, viewpoint, needs and experience.
- They can help prevent costly lawsuits that may result if important information is missing.
- Papers that seem inconsequential can be surprisingly important if the information they contain is complete and effective.

The following important guidelines to make a particular message complete:

3.3.1 Answer all Questions Asked

Whenever responding to an inquiry, the inquiry may for the information or for the product we have to clearly answer the entire question asked. It is always better to make separate paragraph for each query. Try to answer all questions-stated and implied. A prospective customer's reactions to an incomplete reply are likely to be unfavorable. The receiver may think we are trying to hide the weak point of our organization or we are careless in preparing the message. Incomplete message may generate suspicion in the mind of the receiver.

***Examine** the following pairs of sentences where the second is an improvement over the first one in being complete:*

- I did not receive any response for the complaint I lodged.
- I made a complaint to the Branch Manager on March 29, 2014 on the excessive delay at the cash counter. Can I get a response?

3.3.2 Give Something Extra, when Desirable

In some conditions answering only the questions asked may not make a message complete. We have to provide something additional; it seems desirable to provide the additional information. Sometimes you must do more than answer the customer's reaction to an incomplete reply is likely to be unfavorable.

Example: Suppose you are the coordinator of an event, try to cover all the aspects while providing the information such as:

- Direction how to reach the place of event.
- Where is the parking place for the vehicle?
- Date, timing and day of the event.
- Programme schedule of the event.

3.3.3 Checking for the Five "Wh" Questions

Another way to make your message complete is to answer, whenever desirable, the "five Wh questions", who, what, where, when, why and any other essentials, such as how. The five question method is especially useful when you write requests, announcements or other informative messages. Example: While ordering some material from the supplier we have to make clear the following question:

- What material is needed?
- When the required material is needed?
- To whom and where the materials should be sent?
- How the payments of the material will be made and other necessary details.

3.4 CONCISENESS

Conciseness refers to elimination of unnecessary words and inclusion of interesting topics for the recipients. Conciseness refers to saying whatever we want in fewest in possible words without sacrificing the other C qualities. A concise message saves time and expense for both sender and receiver.

A message should be as brief as possible to gain the attention of the receiver. A receiver should not feel that he is going through unnecessary lengthy messages and wasting his time. Conciseness contributes to emphasis. By eliminating unnecessary words, you help make important ideas stand out.

To achieve conciseness, the following points should be considered as suggestions:

3.4.1 Include Only Relevant Facts and Expressions

The effective, concise message should omit not only unnecessarily wordy expression but also irrelevant material. To be sure you include only relevant facts, observe the following suggestions:

- Stick to the purpose or objectives of the message
- Avoid irrelevant words and long-winded sentences
- Omit information obvious to the receiver; do not repeat at length what that person has already known to the receiver.
- Eliminate lengthy introduction, unnecessary explanation, excessive adjectives and prepositions.
- Get the important point tactfully and concisely.

Avoid unnecessary repetition: Repetition induces monotony but sometimes repetition is necessary for emphasizing an idea but when same thing is repeated two or three times without any reason the message becomes wordy and boring. These can be done by sticking to the following points.

(i) *Use shorter name*: use short name after mentioning the long name once. For example, if once you have mentioned "*Sony Manufac-*

turing Share Private Limited Company" once, you can write "*Sony Company*" instead of such a long name.

(ii) *Make use of initials*: Use pronouns or initials rather than repeating long names i.e. for example you should write "AMU" instead of writing "*Arba Minch University*" again and again.

(iii) *Avoid repetition of sentences*: Cut out all needless expressions and repetition of phrases of sentences.

- *Eliminate wordy expressions*: Use single word substitute instead of phrases whenever possible without changing meanings. Examples:

Wordy	Concise
At this time	Now
Due to the fact that	Because
In due course	Soon
In many cases	Often
In most cases	Usually
Under the circumstances	Because

Examples

Wordy: *We hereby wish to let you know that our company is pleased with the confidence you have reposed in us.*

Concise: *We appreciate your confidence*

Wordy: *Please be advised that your admission statement has been received.*

Concise: *Your admission statement has been received.*

Wordy: *In most cases the date of the inquiry is indicated in the upper right corner.*

Concise: *The policy date is in the upper right corner.*

Wordy: *She bought desks that are of the executive type.*

Concise: *She bought executive type desks.*

Wordy: *Please be advised that your admission statement has been received.*

Concise: *Your admission statement has been received.*

3.5 CONSIDERATION

Consideration means that you prepare every message with the recipient in mind and try to put yourself in his place. The interrelationship between sender and receiver profoundly affects the communication. Try to visualize your readers or listeners with their desire, problems, circumstances, emotions, and probable reactions to your requests. Then handle the matter from their point of view. In the broad sense, consideration underlies the other six "C's" of good business communication.

The followings are the points to be considered in order to make the message considerate:

3.5.1 Focus of "You" instead of "I" or "We"

As we know that the primarily our receivers are usually more concerned about themselves than about you or the company you represent. They are more likely to read your message when they see their names and the pronoun "you" rather than "we" or "us". Therefore, in writing letters to others, we have to write from the point of view of the receiver so that our letters will be effective and bring the required outcome immediately.

3.5.2 Show Reader Benefit or Interest in Reader

Whenever possible and true, show how your readers will benefit from whatever the message asks or announces. They will be more likely to react favorably and do what you suggest if you show that the benefits are worth the effort and cost. In situations where the actual direct reader benefit is impossible or irrelevant to the subject matter, the message should at least show interest in and concern for the reader's needs or viewpoint.

3.5.3 Emphasize on the Pleasant and Positive Facts

In many situations we have to say no, disagree, or to say sorry, a straight forward style may hurt the receiver or the client of the organization. The receiver accepts calmly all the regrets, sorry if they are expressed in pleasant manner. To show consideration for your reader or listener is to accent the positive. This means:

(i) Stressing what can be done instead of what cannot be done favorably.

(ii) Focusing on words your recipient can consider favorably.

In other words, a polite, a positive and pleasant no retains the customer's goodwill.

For example:

Negative approach: We are sorry to inform you that we are not able to open your account without photographs.

Positive approach: Thank you for the order, we will open your account immediately as soon as the photographs reach to us.

Applying integrity and Ethics: To be truly considerate, you need also to apply integrity your written and oral messages. Ethics is concerned with what is right human conduct. Codes of ethics provide standards enabling us to determine the fundamental distinction between the right and the wrong human behavior.

3.6 CONCRETENESS

Concreteness of message refers to being more specific, definite, and vivid rather than general. The main benefit of being concrete is obvious that the receiver knows exactly what is required or desired. The other benefit of being concrete is that the reply might be in the same way that may be interrupted by you as the receiver.

The following guidelines will help in composing concrete, and convincing messages:

3.6.1 Using Specific Facts and Figures

Whenever possible use specific, exact, precise statement or figure instead of general words which helps in making your message more concrete.

Examples:

Examples:	Concrete, Precise
1. He is intelligent	His percentage have increased from 84% in SSC to 88% in HSC
2. Eastern Europe is making progress in obtaining investments	In 1990 investments in Eastern Europe were about US $30 million; today that figure has increased by 12%

But sometimes when you don't know the exact figures and want to be concrete you can write as "half the committee was present".

3.6.2 Put Action in Your Verb Instead of Infinitives

To help make messages vivid and specific you can use comparisons and concrete language. Verbs can bring your concreteness back to being alive and more dynamic. Use of verbs especially the active verbs makes your sentence more specific, personal and concise. Even the passive verbs are more useful sometimes when you want to avoid any personal or accusing comments.

3.6.3 Use Vivid Images and Guiding Words

It is better to use comparisons, figurative expression instead of using your opinions and abstract expressions.

3.7 CLARITY

Clarity means getting your message across so the receiver will understand what you are trying to convey. This is difficult due to different communication barriers. We want that person to interpret our words with the same meaning we have in mind. The message must be so clear that even the dullest man in the world should readily understand it. The communicator must be very clear about all the aspects of the idea in his mind and about the purpose for which it is to be communicated. Accomplishing the goal is difficult because as you know, individual experiences are never identical and words may have different meanings to different persons.

Clarity has two versions which are known as *Clarity of thoughts and Clarity of expressions.*

3.7.1 Clarity of Thoughts

It is clear that the communication begins with the generation of idea in the mind of the sender. There should be a great deal of clarity at this stage to make communication effective. The sender must be clear about the idea he wants to express. For instance,

- *What is the objective of the communication?*
- *What is to be communicated?*
- *Which medium will be more effective to communicate the idea?*

3.7.2 Clarity of Expressions

The sender sends the idea through the encoding process. If the encoding is inappropriate the message will be misinterpreted and it will lead to miscommunication. Therefore it becomes very important to be careful while encoding the message. Most of the messages are transmitted with the help of words, sender should be careful of the meanings and in organizing the words.

Here are some specific ways to be considered in the selection of words:

- *Use simple words*: Short and simple words are more effective than difficult and heavy words. Try to avoid difficult words.

Difficult words (avoid them)	Simple words (use them)
Demonstrate	Show
Utilize	Use
Metropolis	City
Terminate	End

- *Use single words*: Use single words rather than long phrases and trite expressions.

Long phrases (avoid them)	Single words (use them)
At all times	Always
As soon as possible	Immediately
Subsequent to	After
Prior to	Before

- *Use concrete expression*: Concrete expressions create visual images that are easy to remember. Therefore instead of using generalized expression. It is better to avoid using opinions or contextual expression.

General expression	Concrete and effective expression
Examination is to start soon The show case is inexpensive	Examination will start on 3rd march. The showcase costs only $ 2000.

- *Avoid jargon and difficult vocabulary*: Jargons are special language of particular trade or profession. No doubt jargons are more effective if used among the persons of same trade or profession, but problem starts when used between the people who are unknown to the jargons or belongs from different trade or profession.
- *Avoid ambiguity*: Ambiguity is often caused by careless use of personnel pronouns, punctuation. Some words also have more areas of meaning. Ambiguity is also caused by indecisive placing of adverbs.

Example: *Person to shopkeeper on phone: Send me two copies of Business India and Femina magazine. The receiver may inquire to the person whether he needs two copies of each or two magazines in total.*

3.8 COURTESY

To build good friendship with our business partners is being courteous in our communication. Courteous message helps to strengthen present business friendship, as well as making new friends. Courtesy is a quality that enables a request to be refused without killing all hope of future business. Courtesy also means replying promptly to all letters. If you feel your correspondent's comments are unfair, try to answer tactfully. In short, the whole letter should have a courteous tone. It is not what you say; it is how you say it. Courtesy stems from sincere you-attitude.

To be courteous, the following guidelines are suggested:

3.8.1 Answer/respond Promptly

In business it is a general practice to respond to a letter immediately at the same day, when it is received. In some cases immediate response may not be possible because it may need the approval of higher authorities or subordinates regarding the matter of the message. In this case you should at least acknowledge to the sender and intimate the reasonable time to send back the reply of the message.

3.8.2 Omit Expression that Irritate, Hurt or Belittle

Some words and expressions are negative in connotation and irritate the receiver. Particularly when they are used with "you" attitude, they become provocative. Expressions like "you failed", "your irresponsible approach" are going to hurt the receiver. The thoughtful business communicator should avoid expression that might offend the receiver.

3.8.3 Be Tactful Instead of Being Blunt

Though few people are intentionally abrupt or blunt, these traits are common cause of discourtesy. Sometimes they stem from mistaken idea of conciseness or from negative person's attitudes. Be tactful instead of being blunt in your correspondence.

3.8.4 Grant and Apologize Good-Naturedly

Whenever you grant a customer's request, begin your letter with the best news first and inject a courteous ungrudging tone. When someone in your organization makes a mistake, you can apologize and correct the error perhaps even before the customer discovers it.

3.8.5 Apologize Sincerely for an Omission/Thank for a Favour

If you have overlooked or failed to do something, express your regrets promptly and sincerely and make amendments for the omission immediately. If some has done a favor to you, acknowledge it promptly and thank the person generously for being kind to you.

3.9 CORRECTNESS

The correctness principle is more than proper grammar, punctuation and spelling. A message may be perfect grammatically mechanically but still lose a customer and fails to achieve a purpose. Though mistakes are never intentional, but even they spoil our image. It is essential that the sender should verify the correctness of the information before transmitting it to the receiver. And before accepting the information for important decision-making, the receiver should clarify his doubts regarding the accuracy and correctness of the message.

Errors in the messages fall in the following categories:

- Mistakes in names, figures, facts, and words.
- Mistakes in punctuation and capitalization
- Mistakes in the level of language

The following points should be considered as suggestions for the correctness:

3.9.1 Use the Right Level of Language

Communication must be correct in tone and style of expression, spelling, grammar, format, contents, statistical information, stress-unstressed, and so on. there should not be any inaccurate statements in the message. Efforts must be made to avoid errors in spellings, punctuations, and so on. The incorrect written documents lower the receivers' confidence in the sender. In the same way, the incorrect statements and other miscellaneous errors of the speaker lower the listeners' confidence in him and it may blemish his image and reliability too. When communication receiver finds one error he suspects that there can also be other errors in the message. Therefore, he starts searching for other mistakes automatically.

3.9.2 Check Accuracy of Figures, Facts and Words

The subject matter of communication must be correct or accurate. The manner in which the message is transmitted must be absolutely correct. Accuracy in writing can be achieved by careful checking and editing. Correctness demands accurate figures, because decisions may go wrong if wrong figures are given. Over writings, erasures, strikeovers, wrong spellings, faulty grammar, poor sentence construction and so an may distract the receiver and lead to misunderstanding.

3.9.3 Send Messages at the Correct Time

Messages should be transmitted and responded at the appropriate time. The information that is outdated is useless and can amount as a futile effort. Since communication is an expensive process, transmitting outdated information becomes wastage of time, money and human resources.

3.9.4 Send Messages in the Correct Style

This is also called the principle of adaptability. We have to adapt the message to the needs of the receiver. We have to keep in mind the educational background, the width of vocabulary, specialized knowledge, the depth of the information required.

Summary

- The major communication principles are Completeness, Conciseness, Consideration, Concreteness, Clarity, Courtesy, and Correctness.
- These communication principles are also known as 7 "C" of communication. These principles are necessary to compose the effective message in communication.
- Completeness requires answering all questions asked and implied. It also means giving something extra when desirable and also checking for five "Wh" questions.
- Conciseness requires including only relevant facts and expressions. It also means avoiding unnecessary repetition.
- Consideration requires adopting the "You" attitude, it also emphasizes on positive, and pleasant facts.
- Concreteness requires applying specific facts and figures and using vivid image and guiding words.
- Correctness of message implies giving correct facts and sending the messages at correct time and in the correct style.
- Clarity of thought and expressions is important in communication so as to not cause any ambiguity.
- Courtesy in communication is important since it result in friendliness with business partners.

Exercises

1. What are the scientific principles for making a communication effective?
2. What do you mean by completeness of the message?
3. Mention the important guidelines to make our message complete.
4. What is conciseness? Mention the point to avoid unnecessary repetition in the message.
5. What is consideration? Give some suggestion to be considerate in your message.
6. How do you express the clarity of thought and clarity of expression
7. What we can do in order to be courteous in our messages?

Self-Check Questions

1. ______ means being specific, definite and vivid.
   (A) Consideration (B) Completeness
   (C) Concreteness (D) Conciseness
   (E) None
2. All statements are true to make the messages considerate, except:
   (A) Use single words (B) Avoid gender bias
   (C) Emphasis on positives (D) Adopt you approach
   (E) None of above
3. Correctness of the message implies:
   (A) Proper grammar and punctuation
   (B) Correct facts
   (C) Correct time
   (D) Correct style
   (E) All of above

Answers

1. C 2. E 3. E

Chapter 4

Types of Communication in Organization

Contents of the Chapter

- Internal and External Communication
- Formal Flow of Communication
- Informal Communication (Grapevine)

Learning Objectives

After finishing this chapter, students should be able to:

- Understand Internal and external communication
- Explain the formal flow of communication
- Explain the informal flow of communication

4.1 INTRODUCTION

Communication plays an important role in almost all aspects of life. Work in business, government or organizations is impossible without communication. People have to communicate internally and externally in order to exchange information, make decisions, talk about new ideas, plans, proposals etc.

No business can develop in the absence of effective internal and external communication. Each organization has its own approach to transmitting information, both within the organization and to the outside world. Depending on where the business communication transpired we can categorize communication into Internal and External.

An exchange of information within an organization is called **Internal communication**. The exchange of information outside the organization is called **External communication.** To exchange information within and outside the organization uses a variety of formal and informal forms of communication that carry the flow of information.

4.2 INTERNAL AND EXTERNAL COMMUNICATION

4.2.1 Internal Communication

Internal communication involves transmission of information within the organization. Internal communication occurs when employees talk to each other, when a supervisor gives a work instruction to subordinate, or when inter-departmental memos are passed. These communication methods include *memos, reports, meetings, face-to-face discussions, teleconference, videoconference, notices,* and so on. Internal communication plays a vital role in achieving the organizational goals and directly matters to company's concern. The internal communication is important to promote harmony within the organization. Internal communication helps in imparting a feeling of cohesion and closeness between employees.

Effective internal communication is important for the following reasons:

- Business has grown in size
- Business activity has become extremely complex and time bound
- Promotes a spirit of understanding and cooperation among employees

4.2.2 External Communication

External communication is communication with people outside an organization. It is the organization's means of establishing contact with the outside word. External environment of the organization are the department and agencies of government, distributors, retailers, competitors, suppliers, customers and so on.

- **Government agencies and departments:** Business organizations are required to deal with regional authorities, foreign trade offices, banks and other financial authorities, income tax office, sales tax office, post office, transport agencies, etc.
- **Distributors, retailers, and customers:** Researches indicate that companies having better communication can sell their brands better. Sales are promoted through persuasion, which is one of the aspect of communication.

Fig. 4.1

External communication could include *business letters, press releases, advertisements, leaflets, invitations, telegrams, telemessages, proposals, etc.* Messages to persons outside the organization can have a far-reaching effect on its standing and ultimate success. The right letter, proposal, or personal conversation can win back a displeased customer, create a desire for a firm's product or service, help negotiate a profitable sale, encourage collections, motivate performance, in general create goodwill.

4.3 FORMAL AND INFORMAL COMMUNICATION

The differentiation of communication is mainly on the basis of situations. Formal communication is used in the situations like public speaking, mass communication, official communication, and so on. Here, language is used more precisely, and more attention is paid to grammar.

Informal communication takes place in case of informal and personal situations. Less attention is paid to structure of language and grammar. To communicate effectively in your workplace, you need to be able to identify and use both formal and informal communication channels.

Every organization has an established pattern structure to carryout its objectives. The managing director passes necessary and relevant information to concerned departmental managers. These managers issue instructions to supervisors, supervisors direct the clerks and operatives. Thus every organization has hierarchical line of authority and communication channel used for transmitting all the written and oral communication. To maintain a healthy flow of information, effective managers use both formal and informal communication channels.

4.3.1 Formal Communication

The formal communication is communication that flows along the organization's lines of authority. Formal channels of communication are intentionally defined and designed by the organization. The formal flow of information follows the official chain of command.

They represent the flow of communication within the formal organizational structure. Formal communication may move vertically or horizontally. Vertical communication flows from subordinates to superiors or from superiors to subordinates. Horizontally communication flows between people of the employee of equal status. Typically, communication flows in four separate directions: **Downward, Upward, Horizontal, and Diagonal.**

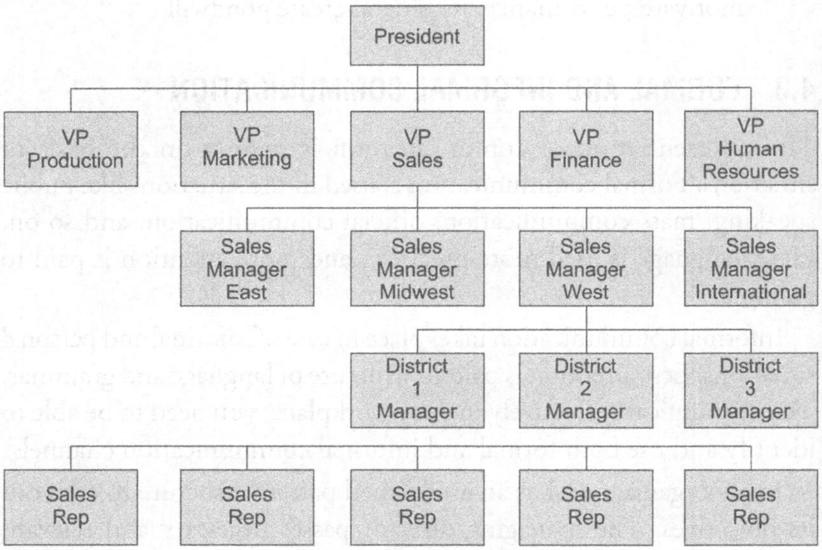

Fig 4.2 Formal communication

Downward Communication

Downward communication is the flow of information from higher officials to lower managerial officials. Communication that involves a message exchange between two or more levels of the organizational hierarchy is called ***Vertical Communication.*** It can involve a manager and a subordinate or can involve several layers of the hierarchy. Vertical communication can flow in a downward or an upward direction.

Formal messages that flow from managers and supervisors to subordinates are called downward communication. Usually, this type of communication involves job directions, assignment of tasks and responsibilities, performance feedback, certain information concerning the organization's strategies and goals. Speeches, policy and procedure manuals, employee handbooks, company leaflets, briefings on the organization's mission and strategies, staff meetings, and job descriptions are all examples of downward communication.

Top management communicates through means as memorandums, conferences, telephone conversations, company's newsletters, policy manuals, bulletin, board announcements and video tapes.

Objectives of the downward communication: Downward communications have the following main objectives:

- To give specific directives about responsibility entrusted to a subordinate.
- To explain policies and organizational procedures.
- To apprise the performance of subordinates.
- To give subordinates information about rationale of their job.

Purpose of downward communication: Most downward communication involves information in one of five categories:

- *Job instructions:* Directions about what to do or how to do it. "When you stock the shelves, put the new merchandise behind the old stock."
- *Job rational:* Explanations of how one task relates to other tasks. Explaining the relationship between a task and other organizational tasks. "We rotate the stock like that so the customer won't wind up with state merchandise."
- *Policy and procedures:* Practice of the organization or rules, regulations and benefits of the organization. "Don't try to argue with unhappy customers. If you can't handle them yourself, call the manager".
- *Feedback:* Information about how efficiently a person is performing. "You are really catching on fast. If you keep up the good work, you'll be an assistant manager by the end of the year".

- *Indoctrination:* Information aimed at motivating employees by impressing the organization's mission upon them and specifying how they should relate to it. Efforts to encourage a sense of mission and dedication to the goals of the organization. "If everyone will put in a little extra effort, we can become the number one producer of X components."

Limitation of downward communication: Downward communication across several levels is prone to considerable distortion. As much as 80% of top management's message may be lost by the time the message reaches five levels below. There are usually three main reasons for the distortion:

- One reason is that faulty message transmission may occur because of sender's carelessness, poor communication skills, and the difficulty of encoding a message that will be clearly understood by individuals at multiple levels.
- Another is that managers tend to overuse one-way communication methods, such as, memos, manuals, and newsletters, leaving little possibility for immediate feedback regarding receiver's understanding.
- Finally, some managers may intentionally or unintentionally filter communications by withholding, screening, or manipulating information.

The major problem with managers and downward communication is their assumption that employees don't need or want to know much about what is going on. Intentional filtering typically occurs when a manager seeks to enhance personal power over subordinates by tightly controlling organizational information.

Essentials of Effective downward communication: The practice of downward communication should not be an ineffective effort, but it has to be effective so that it can achieve its objectives. The following are the essential points to make our downward communication effective:

1. Managers themselves should be well-informed of the objective and activities of their organization. If the manager has adequate information, they will be able to transmit the information to their subordinates in an effective manner.
2. Managers must work according to the decided communication plan. Managers must decide how much information is to be communicated and at what time. It will insure that there is no communication gap.
3. Information must be passed to the correct person in the hierarchy otherwise there will be problem of a smooth flow of downward communication.
4. The orders and instructions can be originated from various levels instead of concentrating the authority at higher level. It will make line of communication shortened, elimination of delays, loss of information and the possibility of distortion will be reduced.

Upward Communication

The flow of information from lower level managerial officers to higher level official is called upward communication. It is the flow of opinions, ideas, complaints, and other kinds of information from subordinates up to managers. It is generated by suggestion systems, grievance procedures, informal and formal meetings, attitude surveys, and exit interviews. Upward communication is important for several reasons.

Managers generally transmit information upwards in the organization relating to job assignment, performance, problems, organizational practices or policies and the methodology for accomplishing tasks. Top level executive depend on lower-level employees to furnish them with accurate, timely reports on problems, emerging trends, opportunities or improvements, and so on.

Usually upward communication is the feedback to downward commemoration. Its major messages include:

- Performance feedback
- Feedback on organizational policies and plans
- Problem solving suggestions

The following types of messages are valuable when communicated upwards:

- What subordinates are doing: highlights of their work, achievements, progress, and future job plan. "We'll have that job done by closing time today".
- Outlines of unsolved work problems on which subordinates now need aid or may require help in the future. "We are still having trouble with the air conditioner in the accounting office".
- Suggestions of ideas for improvements within departments in the organization as a whole. "I think I have figured a way to give people the vacation schedules they want and still keep our staffing up".
- How subordinates think and feel about each other and their jobs, their associates and their organization. "I am having a hard time working with Mr. "X". He seems to think I am mad at him. Or "I am getting frustrated. I have been in the same job for over a year now, and I am seeking for more responsibility".

Importance of upward communication: Upward communications have the following importance:

- **Providing feedback:** Upward communication provides the management with the necessary feedback. It insures that the directives issued to lower level manager have been understood properly or not. Management also gets the valuable information like what is the thinking of employees about the organization and regarding its policies.
- **Outlet for pent up information:** Upward communication gives the opportunity to the employees to express their problems and grievances. In the upward communication employees feel comfortable after addressing their problem with superiors.
- **Constructive suggestions:** Employees also provide some constructive suggestions for the betterment of the organization. These suggestions are sometimes very beneficiary to the organization.

- **Greater harmony and cohesion:** Upward communication acts as a kind of lubricant. It creates greater harmony between the management and the employees.

Methods of upward communication: The business management has become concerned to know about what is going on at several levels below them. They have employed some fairly new techniques like open-door policy, suggestion schemes, etc. and they are still anxious to know any new or advanced method system that can be adopted to get information from the lower ranks.

Forms of upward communication include one – to – one meeting with one's immediate supervisor, staff meetings with supervisors, suggestion systems, grievance procedures, employee attitude survey, progress reports, inquiries, and so on.

Limitations of upward communication: Upward communication has the following limitations/drawbacks.

1. It is subject to substantial distortions for two major reasons.
    - Mobility aspiration
    - Superiors often discourage negative feedback leading to overstated information
2. Bypassing some organizational levels—when employees bypass their immediate supervisor and contact with higher level officials directly, the supervisor will be unfriendly to the employees which leads to poor performance. This may also make top managers lose confidence in the competence of middle level managers. It can lead to information overload to top level managers resulting in filtering and distortion.
3. Upward communication can be unapproachable to many employees.
4. Reluctance or lack of awareness of employees to initiate or respond to upward communication.
5. Some superiors may actively discourage upward communication using their authoritarianism.

Horizontal Communication

Horizontal communication involves exchange of information among individuals on the same organizational level, such as across or within departments. Thus, it generally involves colleagues and peers. Horizontal information informs, supports, and coordinates activities both with in the department and also and interdepartmentally. Considerable horizontal communication in organizations stems from staff specialists, in areas such as engineering, accounting, and human resources management, who provide advice to managers in various departments. Horizontal communication is important to help coordinate work assignments, share information on plans and activities, negotiate differences and develop inter personal support, thereby creating a more cohesive work unit. The more that, individuals or departments within an organization must interact, with each other to accomplish their objectives the more frequent and intense will be the horizontal communication.

Importance of horizontal communication: The Importance of Horizontal communication in an organization is for the following purposes:

- To coordinate task when several employees or departments are each working on part of an important project.
- To solve problems such as how to reduce waste or how to increase the number of items assembled each hour.
- To share information such as an easier way to perform a task or the results of a new survey.
- To solve conflicts such as jealousy or disagreements between co-workers.
- To build rapport: peer support.

Limitation of Horizontal Communication: Three major factors tend to slow down the necessary and, work-related horizontal communication.

- First, competition among individuals or work units can influence individuals to hide information that is potentially damaging to themselves or that may aid others.
- Second, specialization may cause individuals to be concerned mainly about the work of their own unit and to have little appreciation for the work and communication needs of others. For example, scientists in research and development unit that is focused on long-term projects may find it difficult to interrupt their work to help with current customer problems identified by the sales department.
- Third, motivation may be lacking when subordinate's horizontal communication is not encouraged or rewarded.

Diagonal Communication (Cross Channel Communication)

Cross channel communication is the exchange of information among employees in different work units who are neither subordinate nor superior to each other. Staff specialists use cross channel communications frequently because their responsibilities typically involve many departments within the organization. Because they lack line of authority to direct those to whom they communicate, they must often rely on their persuasive skills, as for instance when the human resource department encourages employees to complete a job satisfaction questionnaire. Some organizational structures employ teams comprised of members from different functional areas, even different levels of the hierarchy. With more and more firms reducing the number of management layers and increasing the use of self managed work teams, many workers are being required to communicate with others in different departments and on different levels to solve problems and coordinate work. For instance, a team might be formed from all functional areas (accounting, marketing, operations, and human resources) to work on a specific product project to ensure that all points of view are considered.

Table 4.1 Types of formal communication in organization

	Downward communication	Upward communication	Horizontal (lateral) communication
Definition	Superior to subordinates	Subordinate to superior	Between co workers with different areas of responsibility
Types	Job instructions rations for job organizational policy and procedures, feedback to subordinates, indoctrination to organizational culture	What subordinates are doing, unsolved work problems, suggestions for improvement, subordinate's feelings about job and co-workers	Coordinate tasks, solve problems, share information, manage conflicts, and build rapport
Potential problems	Insufficient or unclear messages, message overload, message distorted as it passes through one or more intermediaries	Superiors may discourage, disregard, or downplay importance of subordinate's messages, supervisors may unfairly blame subordinates for unpleasant news	Competition may occur between employees from different areas of specialization makes understanding difficult information overload discourages contacts physical barriers discourage contact lack of motivation
Potential benefits	Prevention/ correction of employee's errors greater job satisfaction and improved moral	Prevention of new problems and solutions of old ones, increased acceptance of management decisions	Increased cooperation among employees with different duties and greater understanding of organization mission

4.3.2 INFORMAL COMMUNICATION (GRAPEVINE)

Informal communication network ignores formal channels of communication and spreads rumors and gossips at all levels of the organization. Although every business-organization has its formal channels of communication, the informal channel of communication called grapevine also operates in it.

It can be easily found that a large portion of the communication in almost every business house is not formal or pre-planned. The employees communicate through informal channels as they do their jobs. It is neither pre-planned nor deliberately motivated by the management. It is neither written nor documented or recorded. Therefore, it refers to any communication that takes place outside the prescribed and preplanned channels of formal communication. It is not set with the lines of organizational hierarchy. As it has no set rules and regulations, it is not confined to a particular direction. It just spreads like a grapevine.

4.3.3 Importance of Informal Communication (Grapevine)

The structure of the grapevine is not so well defined, as that of the formal channels; it should not be taken for its weakness. The messages flowing through grapevine have greater speed than that of the messages flowing through the formal channels.

The employees communicate through grapevine, not because they are compelled to communicate but because they earnestly want to communicate with their associates.

Informal communication can serve several useful functions:

1. **Confirming:** Some informal communication confirms formal messages. You have probably heard this sort of confirmation yourself. The boss is really serious about cutting down on long-distance calls this time. "I heard him yelling about it when I walked past his office."
2. **Expanding:** Information communication can fill in the gaps left by incomplete formal messages. You might say to an experienced

co-worker "the invitation to the office party says 'casual dress' what it means—jeans and T- shirt or sport coat and tie?"

3. **Expediting:** Informal networks can often deliver messages more quickly than official channels can. Canny job hunters, for example, often use personal contacts to learn about openings within an organization before the vacancies are published.
4. **Contradicting:** Sometimes informal networks contradict official messages. You might learn from a friend in accounting that the deadline for purchases on this year budget is not as firm as it sounded in the controller's recent memo.
5. **Circumventing:** Informal contacts can sometimes help you bypass official channels that are unnecessary cumbersome and time consuming. Your tennis partner who works in duplicating might sneak in an occasional rush job for you instead of putting it at the end of the line.
6. **Supplementing:** Sometimes even management realizes that informal communication can get the job done better than the more formal variety can. Paradoxical a it seems, many companies elevate informal communication to an official policy by encouraging open, unstructured contacts between people from various parts of the organization.

4.3.4 Limitations of Grapevine

1. The grapevine may carry some degree of error in it.
2. The baseless, imaginary and non-factual messages may prove harmful to the organization.
3. Often the employees feed the grapevine with self-serving information. They add to the facts rather than simply report.
4. The grapevine often carries incomplete information, which leads to misunderstanding of the receiver.
5. The communicator does not take the responsibility of the message.

6. Sometimes the grapevine spreads the message so swiftly that it causes damage to the organization.

4.3.5 How to use the Grapevine for management purpose

The management can use grapevine to supplement the formal channels of communication. Though it carries some degree of error and distortion, efforts can be made to correct it. Ignoring the grapevine is nothing but to ignore a valuable source of communication. The management can eliminate its negative consequences and, at the same time, it can nourish its positive benefits. The managers have to learn to manage and control it.

The following suggestions can be taken by the managers of the organizations to control grapevine:

1. The management can open up all the channels of organizational communication to present the facts positively before the employees and thereby can fight the negative messages.
2. Better job design and better quality of work life can easily bring the grapevine under the control of the management.
3. The negative consequences can be easily eliminated if the management is successful in creating trust-relationship with the employees.
4. The rumors flourish beyond limits when the employees are not well informed by the management regarding the policies, objectives and the work procedure of the organization. The inadequate access to information and the feeling of insecurity is the reasons behind the negative outcomes of the grapevines. The managers must give their employees an adequate access to information and the feeling of security.
5. The rumors spread when the situations are unpredictable, unstructured, unplanned and are beyond the control of a person or the persons who are involved in them. Therefore, the best way to manage and control it is to provide accurate and substantial information of the situations to the employees. The managers

should pick up the false rumors and disperse them by providing correct information.

6. Before taking any decision or action, the managers must consider its possible effects on the informal groups and systems in the organization.
7. In the formal activities of the organization, the management should avoid threatening the informal groups, which are responsible in spreading the grapevine effectively.
8. The management should find out the people in the informal groups who are more active on grapevine. These people should be accurately and adequately informed so that the false rumors causing excitement and insecurity do not spread among the employees.
9. The management should remember that the workplace community is maintained not only by the work itself but also by the informal human relationships. Therefore, the manager should honestly try to integrate their interests with those of the informal groups.

Despite the fact that grapevines sometimes create difficulties when they carry gossip and false rumors, they are a fact of life in organizations and it is unrealistic for managers to think that they can eliminate grapevine. The type of information the grapevine carries depends on the "health" of the organization. If an organization's managers are fairly open with employees and send all necessary information through formal channels, the grapevine usually caries only personal interest items.

Summary

- In organizational context, communication can be broadly classified depending on the framework. It is classified as internal and external communication.
- Internal communication is a communication that takes place among and between individuals in an organization.
- The exchange of information outside the organization is called external communication.

- Internal communication can be further classified into formal and informal communication.
- The formal communication is classified as horizontal, vertical, downward and upward.
- The informal communication is grapevine, which is not structured by the organization.
- Each kind of formal communication has its own advantages and disadvantages. As a result organization uses a combination, in fact all types of communication.

Exercises

1. What do you understand by internal and external communication in an organization?
2. What are the methods of external communication which organizations use and with whom?
3. Explain the objectives of the downward communication.
4. What are the limitations of downward communication?
5. Explain the importance of upward communication.
6. What is horizontal communication? Explain its importance.
7. Explain clearly the meaning of the term "Grapevine'
8. Explain how grapevine can serve organization in useful manner.

Self-Check Questions

1. Horizontal communication is used for
   (A) Coordinating tasks (B) Sharing information
   (C) Solving problems (D) Resolving conflict
   (E) All
2. Individuals from different units and different organizational level communicate each other in ______________
   (A) Downward communication (B) Upward communication
   (C) Horizontal communication (D) Diagonal communication
   (E) All
3. The following messages are valuable when communicated upward, Except

(A) What subordinates are doing
(B) Feedback on employee's performance appraisal
(C) Suggestions for improvements with in departments
(D) How subordinates think about their job
(E) None

4. Most downward communication involves the following information. Except
   (A) Job instructions related to specific tasks
   (B) Rules and regulations of the organizations
   (C) Outlines of unsolved problems on which subordinates need aid
   (D) Explaining the relationship between a task and other organizational tasks
   (E) None
5. Among the following which one is not true abut grapevine?
   (A) Does not flow along the official path
   (B) Communication takes place without task requirement
   (C) It is not deliberately designed
   (D) It is intentionally defined and designed by the organization
   (E) None

Answers

1. E   2. D   3. B   4. D   5. D

CHAPTER 5

Public Relations

Contents of the Chapter

- Definitions of Public Relations
- Activities of Public Relations
- Public Relations Strategy
- Public Relations Process
- Profile of Public Relations Officer
- Work Assignments of Public Relations Officer
- Media Relations
- Achieving Objectives
- Managing Crisis with Media
- Hints for Writing Press release
- Handling Press Questions

Learning Objectives

After finishing this chapter, students should be able to:

- Explain Public Relation (PR) concept and its importance
- Define the public relations
- Explain the major activities of the public relations
- Understand the public relation strategy and process
- Develop better media relations

5.1 INTRODUCTION

Public Relations (PR) primarily concerns enhancing and maintaining the image for businesses, non-profit organizations, events or high-profile people, such as celebreties and politicians. Public relation is deliberate, planned and sustained effort to establish and maintain mutual understanding between an organization and its public. The public of the organization include all the people who come into the contact such as customers, dealers, suppliers, investors, transporters, bank and media people.

Public relations are used to build rapport with employees, customers, investors, voters, or the general public. There are a number of public relations disciplines falling under the corporate communications, such as analyst relations, media relations, investor relations, internal communications and labor relations. Most of them include the aspect of peer review to get liability.

Other Public Relations disciplines include:

- **Financial Public Relations** – providing information mainly to business reporters
- **Consumer/Lifestyle Public Relations** – gaining publicity for a particular product or service, rather than using advertising
- **Crisis Public Relations** – responding to negative accusations or information
- **Industry Relations** – providing information to trade bodies
- **Government Relations** – engaging government departments to influence policymaking

5.2 DEFINITIONS OF PUBLIC RELATIONS

The first World Assembly of Public Relations Associations, 1978 defines "*Public relation is the art and social science of analyzing trends, predicting their consequences, counseling organizational leaders, and implementing planned programs of action, which will serve both the organization and the public interest.*"

Others define public relations as:

- "*Public Relations is the deliberate, planned and sustained effort to establish and maintain mutual understanding between an organization and its publics.*"- Institute of Public Relations, USA
- "*Public Relations is the attempt by information persuasion and adjustment to engineer public support for an activity, cause, movement or institution.*" - Edward L. Bernays
- "*Public Relations is a combination of philosophy, sociology, economics, language, psychology, journalism, communication and other knowledge into a system of human understanding.*"- Herbert M. Baus
- "*The Management function which gives the same organized and careful attention to the asset of goodwill as is given to any other major asset of business.*" - John W. Hill

5.3 ACTIVITIES OF PUBLIC RELATIONS

The major activities of the public relation department include:

- Publicity campaigns
- Maintaining relations with press
- Arranging seminars and conferences
- Arranging press conferences and issuing press releases
- Dealing with public inquiries
- Making questionnaires and conducting opinion pools
- Providing information to public and acquiring feedback
- Maintaining cordial relationship with government officials
- Publishing house journals and bulletins
- Getting direct touch with the customers

5.4 PUBLIC RELATIONS STRATEGY

Public relations strategy is to be developed for the effective implementation of public relation goals and objective. The process of strategy begins with planning the followings:

(a) **Determining the targeted area:** The first stage of the public relation strategy is to find out the targeted result areas, where focus has to be given. The area should be determined.

(b) **Identify roles:** After determining the targeted area of focus, the roles should be identified

(c) **Selecting and setting objectives:** Once the roles have been identified, public relation officer has to set the objectives.

(d) **Action plan**: Public relation officer has to prepare action plans concerning to programming, development, budgeting, fixing responsibility and establishing rules and procedures.

Rice and Paisley also suggested guidelines for planning a successful public relation operation, which are as follows:

(i) Assessment of the needs, goals and capabilities of target audiences

(ii) Systematic campaign planning and production

(iii) Continuous evaluation

(iv) Complementary roles of mass media and interpersonal communication

(v) Selection of appropriate media for target audiences.

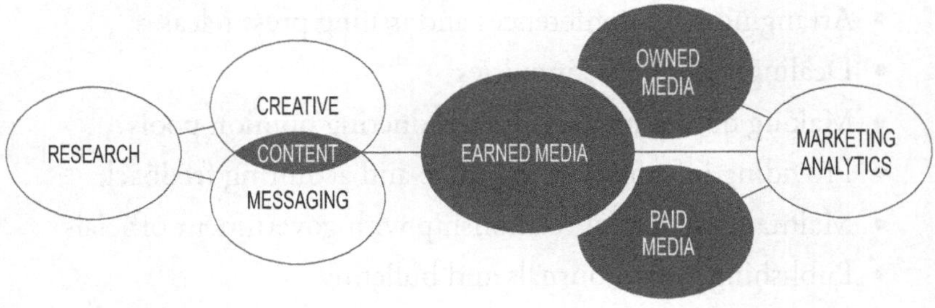

5.5 PUBLIC RELATIONS PROCESS

Public relations process is the act that outlines the various steps to be undertaken before implementing any program or events to ensure the success of a program, while public interests (internal and external) are not affected (Newsom and Turk, 2004). **The process**

of public relations takes place in seven phases which are as follows:

The first phase of public relations process is identifying and listing out the information or message to the communicator.

The second phase of public relations process is to ascertain the existing image or awareness level about the issue in the target group or common public.

The third phase of public relations process is to develop of communication objectives and priorities.

The fourth phase of public relations process deals with developing the message and choosing the media to transit.

The fifth phase of public relations process is the implementation of the message and media, coordination or the dissemination of message.

The sixth phase of public relations process is communication process to check whether message reached properly and the expected action or behavior or knowledge on image factors.

The seventh phase of public relations process in case the message did not reach properly is to identify the reason for the ineffectiveness and rectification of the same and disseminates the revised message.

5.6 PROFILE OF A PUBLIC RELATIONS OFFICER

In order to achieve the goal of the public relations the public relations officer is expected to have the following profile:

Help with the public relations aspects of decisions

Skill in communicative principles and in enlarging understanding of the organization

Loyalty

Inspiration to help all members of the department / division to do their best cheerfully

Influence in restraining other members from saying or doing anything detrimental to the organization's welfare

5.7 WORK ASSIGNMENTS OF PUBLIC RELATIONS OFFICER

(a) *Writing:* News releases, newsletters, correspondence, reports, speeches, booklet texts, radio and television copy, film scripts, trade paper and magazine articles, institutional advertisements, product information, and technical materials.

(b) *Editing:* Special publications, employee newsletters, shareholder reports, and other communications directed to internal and external publics.

(c) *Media relations and placement:* Contacting news media, magazines, sunday supplements, freelance writers, and trade publications with the intent of getting them to publish or broadcast news and features about or organized by the organization. Responding to media requests for information or spokesperson.

(d) *Special events:* Arranging and managing press conferences, convention exhibits, open houses, anniversary celebrations, fund-raising events, special observances, contests, and award programmes.

(e) *Speaking:* Appearing before groups and arranging platforms for others before appropriate audiences by managing a speaker's bureau.

(f) *Production:* Creating communications using multimedia knowledge and skills; including art, photography, and layout for brochures, booklets, reports, institutional advertisements, and periodical publications; recording and editing audio and video tapes; and preparation of audio visual presentations.

(g) *Research:* Gathering intelligence – enabling the organization to plan programmes responsive to its public's and problem situations, monitoring public relations programme effectiveness during implementation, and evaluating programme impact.

(h) *Programming and counseling:* Determining needs, priorities, goals, publics, objectives, and strategies. Collaborating with management or clients in a problem solving process.

(i) *Training:* Working with executives and other organizational representatives to prepare them for dealing with the media, and for making presentations and other public appearances. In service staff development.

(j) *Management:* Administering the operation of the public relations function – personal, budget and programmes.

5.8 MEDIA RELATIONS

A Media relation takes several outward appearances in most companies, which starts from publicity to crisis management. It consists of investor relations as well, particularly at smaller companies. While large companies have positions dedicated exclusively to media relations, this is not always the case at smaller companies, where the responsibility is part of another executive's duties. Even if there is a media relations group, every executive and manager has a degree of media relations responsibility at all times, and at certain times can be at the center of a media relations campaign or crisis. For this reason, it is good for all executives and managers to know how to do good media relations.

A company's media relations activities are managed through public relations, external affairs or communications department for handling any situations. One person handles all inquiries from the press, and manages all efforts to gain attention from the press for positive publicity on behalf of the company. This person is most often called the director of media relations, and he/she is usually the **spokesperson** for the company as well.

While the responsible person for this activity handles routine queries (quarterly results, questions about press releases, etc.), there are others who can and will speak to the press in specific circumstances. These incidences can be positive. For example record profits, successful product launching, and a beneficial tie up with well brand or it may negative such as layoffs, product failure, and stockholder court case. These people will be selected, trained and coordinated by the director of media relations and the head of the department. Good media relations mean the company can maximize the positive effects of news coverage and minimize the damage from negative news coverage.

5.8.1 Achieving Objectives

To achieve the above objectives the public relations officer requires the followings:

- **A Close Relationship with the CEO***:* The person responsible for media relations must have a good working relationship with the Chief Executive Officer. In most companies, the only way to know what is going to happen ahead of time is to find out from the CEO. Fortunately, the CEO typically has a very deep interest in how she/he, her/his management team, and the company look in the newspapers, so that kind of relationship usually comes with the province.
- **Good Working Relationships with the Management Team***:* Media training is important for those who will deal with the media on a regular basis, or when crisis comes. An environment of trust between the director of media relations and senior managers is vital, particularly when third parties (media training, PR companies) become part of any campaign.
- **Good Relationships with the Press:** Whether it is local press, national press, industry press, or all three that matter to the company, the director of media relations must have the knowledge of who writes what for whom, what they have written in the past, and how to contact them. Knowing who covers what at a paper is partly just a matter of courtesy, and partly a vital component of the company's credibility with reporters. Subscription services provide the most up to date listings of reporters, with addresses and phone numbers, and that's a good start. But it is up to the director of media relations to build that information into a relationship. Frequent contact is the best insurance; because reporters change assignments and even jobs with some regularity.

5.8.2 Crisis Management

The reason it is called "Crisis Management" because there are ways of handling even the worst events. There is no escape, but following the guidelines below can minimize the intensity and the duration of the pain for the company, the managers, and the stockholders.

- **Collect all the information:** In crisis period, a media relations person collects all the necessary information to assess the multiple levels at which damage could occur. Later, this information will be used in framing the company's response, but it is used immediately to determine how wide and deep the damage is or will be. What will this news do to sales? Will it have an effect on ongoing negotiations? What will be the reactions of stockholders and analysts who cover the company? The aim is to construct a response that acknowledges the mistakes that have been made and which lays the foundation for the rebuilding process.
- **Finding the reality:** Getting the truth from the people within the company is difficult. Asking tough questions can bring out fear in colleagues. But getting the truth out there, in the public arena, is an important step in recovery. And the acknowledgement must be complete. The goal is to build credibility during a period when many angry people do not want to believe a thing the company says, so there can be no further negative disclosure that undercut what has been said.
- **Framing the response:** The writer of the response (which will take the form of a press release or a press conference) ties every admission to the image of the company that he/she hopes will emerge. When the company's spokesperson says, "We did not tell the truth," there is the implied message that the company did tell the truth in the past, and that principle will again guide it in the future. Every lie, mistake, or whatever is unusual will be corrected. The admission does not try to make this point immediately, but rather it sets the stage for a new company structure. Bit by bit, good media relations moves the company as a whole and most of the employees away from blame and away from involvement in the problem.
- **Create talking points:** Once the response is drafted, it must be approved by the CEO and by senior management. When this

approval is granted, the next step is to prepare talking points. The talking points keep everyone who talks to the media consistent in their responses on message, and helps the company "speak with one voice" in much the way it does when there is a single spokesperson. Having senior managers contradicting each other in the paper or on TV is disastrous during a crisis

- **Internal announcement:** This message for employees contains the same information as was in the press release/press conference. It addresses employees as a specific audience and can ask for their continued trust. The internal announcement should match with the press release or the press conference.
- **Working the story:** Public relation firms like Edelman Worldwide and Hill & Knowlton offer such training, and it is worth seeking. They also offer crisis management services, and they should be considered if the crisis extends beyond the company's locality, or if the company needs expertise beyond its own capabilities. For example, if the company does not do government relations on an ongoing basis, but the crisis demands that it have the support of elected officials, it should hire a good PR company.
- **The rebuilding process:** Media relations should be alert for the point at which the crisis, which has kept building, now begins to subside. This is the signal to begin the rebuilding process. Signs to look for are stories that unwillingly give the company credit for honesty, or which note that no more negatives has emerged since the original admissions. It is good for executives to put themselves in the role of the media relations executive even if that is never their primary responsibility, because it is always part of their responsibility. Media opportunities and media crises come without warning, and the only way to deal with them is to be prepared ahead of time. The more responsible the position is within a company, the greater the responsibility is to anticipate the needs of media relations.

5.8.3 Hints for Writing Press Release

Whenever the organization starts writing the press release they have to be very careful in doing so. The following points should be considered for writing the effective press release:

- First paragraph should be sharp and crisp
- Prepare small paragraphs
- Avoid redundant expressions
- Choose positive rather than reactive headline
- Avoid uncommon words
- Avoid jargon and the use of initials
- Check the spelling of people and place names
- Type on one side in double spacing and leave a good margin
- Better give, one page 25 lines write up
- Check the appearance of the information and make it attractive
- Put the date and time and mention contact person and telephone number for clarifications if needed

5.8.4 Handling Press Questions

The representative of the organization or company should have confidence to face the media while handling the press question, lack of confidence may destroy the event or it may not be impressive as it is expected. The representative should have the ability to think and react on the question instantly and handle the question tactfully. The representative should have authority and crisis management skills. We can summarize this in the points, the representative should:

- Be Confident
- Have the ability to think and react on questions instantly
- Be Tactful
- Have Authority, and
- Have Crisis management skill

Doyle's Communications Chart

Group	Objective	Management Action	PR. Action	Communication channel	Type of Message
General Public	Good-will Respect Support	Conduct business in public interest Support community projects	Survey Plan Communicate Evaluate	Mass media Mail replies Phant-tour folders	Institutional ads News on basic information about company
clients*	Seller	Produce good product or service	Survey Plan Communicate Evaluate	Mass Media Trade Journals Direct mail Films	Sale ads Product news Institutional ads
Customers- Employees. Management ranks	Loyalty Goodwill Efficient Production Good morale	Help employees find work satisfaction. self respect run	Survey Plan Communicate Evaluate	Company Publications Bulletin boards Mass media Direct mail Film	News and features about company and individual employees and employee employee Institutional ads.
Stock holders bankers counsellors	Operating Capital Confidence Good will	Good Management	Survey Plan Communicate Evaluate	Company publication Newsletter Mass media	Progress reports Fixture plans Financial reports Institutional Ads

Group	Objective	Management Action	PR Action	Communication Channel	Type of Message
Government officials. civil leaders	Goodwill support Favourable decisions	Conduct business in public interest Support community projects	Survey Plan Communicate Evaluate	Personal contact Speeches Mass media Films	News about company progress and plans Editorials Institutional ads
Press, Radio-TV	Respect Confidence **in** statements	"Open door" policy Truth	Survey Plan Communicate Evaluate	Personal meetings Memos Press tours General news tips	Shop talk Back- ground on company news
Educators	Respect Support Goodwill	Host Plant visits Serve on PTA boards, etc.	Survey Plan Communicate Evaluate	Personal contact Speeches Direct mail	Offers to help educators

Source: *Effective Public Relations 6th Edition, Scott M.Cutlip, Allen H.Center, Glen M. Brooms Pg.No.358*

A Comparative Evaluation of the Media of Advertising

S. No.	Media Factors	News Papers	Magazines	Direct Mail	Radio	Cinema	Outdoor
1.	Circulation	Widest	Limited circulation	Restricted to the member of mailings contacted	Good Circulation	Restricted to local population	Limited to local circulation
2.	Degree of Selectivity	Generally universal In appeal. It permits Regional and linguistic Selectivity	Greater degree of selectivity	Higher degree of selectivity	Restricted regional and linguistic selectivity	Restrited local selectivity	Local Selectivity
3.	Audience	Generally very large but limited to those who can read and subscribe	Limited in scope	Limited to a live mailing list which should constantly be reviewed	Limited be those who possess radio and who tune into the programme	Limited to cinema going population	Limited to local people
4.	Timeliness	Message may be varied at short notice Current events may be capatilised	Lack of timeliness absence of news value	Highest degree of timeliness selection of the right time and right message possible	Restricted Timeliness depending upon programme planning	Timeliness but at a higher cost	Uneconomic timeliness
5.	Flexibility of size design layour and colour	High degree of flexibility	Less flexibility	Highest degree of flexibility	Restricted flexibility depending on the availability of time	Highest degree of flexibility but at proportionately higher costs	Good Degree of flexibility but uneconomical

S. No.	Media Factors	News Papers	Magazines	Direct Mail	Radio	Cinema	Outdoor
6.	Life	Very limited life	Longer life commensurate with frequency of issue and use for reference	Subsequently longer life dependings upon the use fullness of the literature	Limited Life	Very short Lived unless repeated very frequently	Longer life
7.	Repetitive value	Message may be repeated every day and adopted to the day's need	Repititive value restricted to frequency of publication	Repititive value depends on frequency of mailing	Quick repetition	May be repeated in every show but not to the same audience	Seen every time prospect passes by it
8.	Effective ness	Well planned News paper Advertisement is very effective in locating new customers buying in market and supporting	Very Effective in case of technical goods has also the good will of the publication to support	Most effective because of the personal touch undivided attention elaborate explanations	Less effective because of shorter memory and shorter messages	Very effective Because audio visual value may be made effective by use of cartoons and elaborate explanation	High memorizing value
9.	Secrecy	No Secrecy can be maintained because of universal appeal	No secrecy competitors also read it	Privacy and secrecy may easily be maintained	No secrecy	No secrecy	No secrecy

S. No.	Media Factors	News Papers	Magazines	Direct Mail	Radio	Cinema	Outdoor
10.	Economy	Moderate coast per advertisement to numbers contacted	Higher cost per advertisement but less over-all costs	Cost depend upon the size of the mailing list	Costlier	Moderate cost as a whole but higher per contract costs	Cheap on the whole but higher per contract costs
11.	Suitability	Suitable for all types of goods having wide market and needing constant explorations	Suitable for specific goods according to the nature of the magazine	Very suitable for articles having a well defined limited and enlightened tened marked	Suitable for articles of daily use in wide demand	Most suitable for local consumption goods	Very suitable to make a brand image

Source: *Advertising: Principles and Practice, Chunawalla.Sethia*

Case Study: Media Relations

Local Story Makes National News

An article in the *San Diego Tribune* about Fary Moini, a member of the Rotary Club of La Jolla Golden Triangle, California, USA, caught the eye of a producer from *NBC Nightly News*. After reading it, he contacted the club to discuss doing a story about her. Honoring Moini as a "hometown hero," the article praised her extraordinary work to aid Afghan refugees in Pakistan and Afghanistan and highlighted her Rotary experience and its impact on others in the world. In the story, she said, "I belong to a great organization, Rotary International, and with their encouragement, with their support, I was able to do these small things with love."

After gathering background information, the *NBC Nightly News* produced a human interest piece featuring Moini's efforts as part of the show's "Making a Difference" series. The 2:40-minute broadcast was seen by millions of viewers. It focused on how Moini worked with her Rotary club to raise US$250,000 to construct a school equipped with a science lab, library, and computer room for 2,000 children in war-ravaged Jalalabad, Afghanistan. The NBC team followed her to Afghanistan and shot footage of the opening of the mixed-gender school.

Moini was interviewed during the piece and was able to share Rotary with the world, all of which provided great coverage for Rotary and allowed viewers to see how Rotarians are active in both their communities and around the world.

And, it all began with local news coverage.

Critical Thinking

How well selected media for communicating message can reach to the targeted audience in the effective manner?

Summary

- Public Relations is deliberate, planned and sustained effort to establish and maintain mutual understanding between an organization and its public.
- The public of the organization include customers, dealers, suppliers, investors, transporters, banks and media people.
- Public Relations is the attempt by information persuasion and adjustment to engineer public support for an activity, cause, movement or institution.
- The major activities of the public relations department include publicity campaigns, maintaining relations with press, arranging seminars and conferences, arranging press conferences and issuing press releases, dealing with public inquiries, getting direct touch with the customers.
- Work assignment of public relations officer is writing, editing, media relations and placement, arranging special events, speaking production, research programming and counseling and providing trainings.
- A company's media relations activities are managed through a public relations, external affairs or communications department for handling any situations.

Exercises

1. What is public relations? Explain the other discipline of public relations.
2. Define public relations.
3. What are the activities of public relations?
4. Explain phasewise the process of public relations.
5. Explain pointwise the working assignment of the public relations officer.
6. What is a media relation?
7. What is expected from public relations officer in order to achieve the objectives of media relation?
8. What are the points to be considered while writing a press release?
9. What are the qualities required in public relations representative to handle the press questions?

Self-Check Questions

1. Identify the wrong statement regarding public relation
   - (A) Concern with enhancing and maintaining the image of the business.
   - (B) Is a deliberated, planned effort to establish mutual understanding betweenorganization and its public.
   - (C) Concern with high profile people only
   - (D) Used to build rapport with general people
   - (E) None of the above
2. Definition "The Management function which gives the same organized and careful attention to the asset of goodwill as is given to any other major asset of business." has been given by:
   - (A) John W. Hill
   - (B) Institute of PR, USA
   - (C) Edward L.bernays
   - (D) Hermert M. Baus
   - (E) None of the Above
3. To achieve the above objectives the public relations officer requires
   - (A) A close relationship with the CEO
   - (B) Good working relationships with the management team
   - (C) Good relationships with the press
   - (D) Option A & C only
   - (E) All of the above
4. Identify among the options that is not the work assignment of public relations:
   - (A) Writing and editing
   - (B) Arranging Special events
   - (C) Media relations and placement
   - (D) Production and research
   - (E) None of the above
5. The major activities of the public relations department includes
   - (A) Publicity campaigns
   - (B) Maintaining relations with press.

(C) Arranging seminars and conferences.

(D) Arranging press conferences and issuing press releases.

(E) All of the Above

Answers

1. C	2. A	3. E	4. E	5. E

CHAPTER 6

Impact of Technological Advancement on Business Communication

Contents of the Chapter

- Communication Networks
- Communication in a "Network" Organization: Facing New Realities
- Intranet and Usages of Intranet for Communication
- Internet
- E-mails
- Short Message Service (SMS)
- Teleconferencing
- Videoconferencing

Learning Objectives

After finishing this chapter, students should be able to:

- Explain the Communication network
- Explain the Advancement in Technology for communication
- Know about the intranet and its advantages to organizations
- Describe about the Internet, E-mails and SMS technology
- Understand the communication technology like Teleconferencing and Video-conferencing

6.1 INTRODUCTION

Thinking of conducting modern business without the use of communication technology is unimaginable. In 19th century, the use of technological communication became extensive. These technology based communication tools created a major insurrection in business practices.

Technological developments have eliminated two great obstructions to communication—time and distance. Some most dramatic changes have occurred in communication and information technology, which, of course had a major impact on the communication within the office. The Continental PIR Communication Chairman and CEO, Christopher H. Bunting, believes that leading companies place a high priority on both internal and external communication.

There are hundreds of communications and information technology tools and software programs that aid the communication process. From planning and developing to information gathering, analysing and organizing, writing and editing, presenting, storing, and distributing or sharing, technological tools can simplify and expedite the process. These tools can aid in preparing a written communication, such as letter, memo, or report, an oral presentation or any other type of communication project whether we are working on an individual project or group project.

6.2 COMMUNICATION NETWORKS

When we communicate with those above us, below us, or around us, we are establishing *Communication Networks*. These may be *formal* channels or *informal* channels.

Within the organization, there are usually four types of networks:

1. **Wheel:** A wheel network exists when there is a supervisor with a number of subordinates reporting directly without consultation or links with each other.
2. **Chain:** In a chain communication network information is passed sequentially to the next employee above or below in the line of authority.

3. **Circle:** The circle is a three level hierarchy with the lowest level of employees communicating with each other and directly with the person on the next level. That level then reports directly to the higher level. Communication also occurs downwards between the levels.
4. **Star or the all channel network:** It is more an ideal than a real: Every member of the organization is able to communicate directly as an equal with every other member. Some committees are examples of all channel (star) networks.

The most structured is the wheel; the least structured is the star, where opportunities for feedback are greatest and morale is usually the highest.

6.3 COMMUNICATION IN A "NETWORK" ORGANIZATION: FACING NEW REALITIES

Today Information Technology provides the communication and analytical power that organizations need for conducting their businesses and managing business comfortably at global level. Organizations use information and communication technology to coordinate their worldwide network of suppliers, distributors and consumers. Organizations have developed global information system that can track orders, their delivery status and payments at any time.

It is becoming clear that no small group at the top can provide the leadership needed for an entire organization of any size in the information age. The demands on the total organization are too great for a few people at the top to call all the shots.

Today, better-informed customers, rapid change, and aggressive competition from global competitors demand empowered employees exercising leadership at every level of the organization. This is not possible without a radical restructuring of the traditional sequential model of organizational communication. There have been three pervasive patterns that will no longer work in knowledge-based organizations which are as follows.

1. The primary flow of information was vertical—within departmental walls that were often impermeable,
2. Information was hoarded and used as a source of power over others, and
3. People at the top often withheld crucial strategic information from those lower in the organization in the belief they couldn't handle it.

The restrictive and regulatory function of the traditional sequential model of communication is no longer effective in ensuring the timely delivery of the right kind of information to the right people at all levels of the modern organization.

The new, contemporaneous communication model is evolving—it is goal oriented and emphasizes an interactive process that supports simultaneous and spontaneous communication. Since communication is a critical element in organizational design, a new type of "network" organization is evolving, with formal and informal interactive communication structures at all units and levels. As the environment becomes more dynamic, the general trend is for organizations to move from the mechanistic structure to organic structure in order to remain competitive.

6.3.1 Advancement in Technology for Communication

Communication systems today are indistinguishably linked to computers. Even nowaday's mobile telephone has all the features like computer in it. In the fast changing environment global scenario project leader needs to be able to exchange the information quickly. Electronic communication is the only possible way to share the information in the fastest manner and influence the today's business world. Organizations best able to collect, tabulates, manipulates, store and share information among organizational members are the strongest competitors in this information ages.

The internet, e-mail, voice mail, faxes, pagers, and other wireless tools and technologies not have revolutionized the way people communicate. These Technological advances only being new and better tools to the workplace but also increase the speed, frequency, and reach of communication. People from opposite ends of the world can work together effortlessly, 24 hours a day. Moreover, advances in technology make it possible for more and more people to work away from the office-in cars, airports, hotels and at home.

6.4 INTRANET

Intranetware is an evolving concept which allows multi-users can have access to the same information. Intranetware provides a mechanism that helps users coordinate and keep track of on-going projects together. Intranet is also called *Collaborative software.*

A fundamental component of Intranetware is e-mail, because e-mail is used to notify team members, obtain responses and send alerts. Intranetware is comprehensive. Intranetware also includes document sharing and document management, group calendaring and scheduling, group contact and task management, threaded discussions, text chat, data conferencing and audio and videoconferencing.

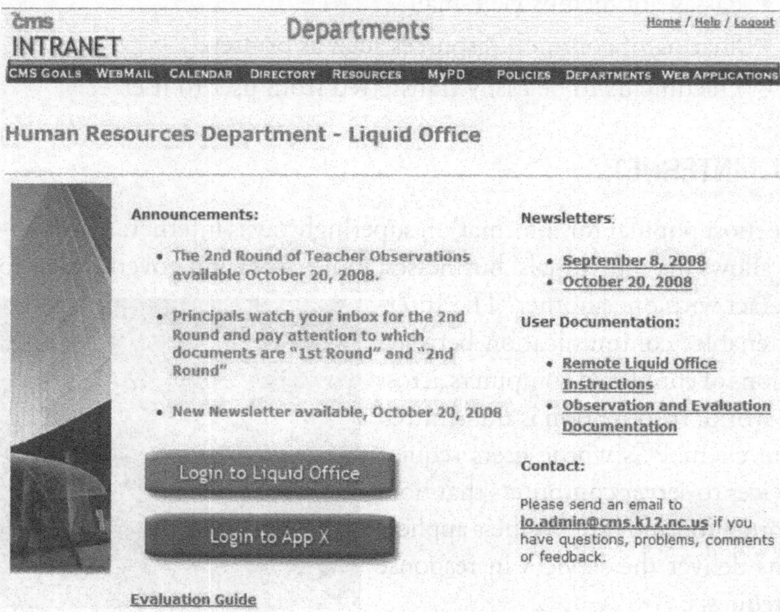

Source: www.digitalpodcast.com

6.4.1 Usages of Intranet for Communication

Modern companies use intranets to communicate a wide range of information among their employees. For example Cisco Systems uses its intranet to provide new employees to have quick access to all necessary information about the company structure, their company policies, and about their current future and past operation.

Intranets can also be used to provide access to all employees to get a copy of minutes of meeting, important presentations that might be reprocessed by different sales people, and information on the current status of manufacturing operations and so on. In a nutshell, any business document carrying information that might be useful can be easily shared between organizational employees.

Intranets are particularly useful to organizations because they allow:

- Sharing of programs
- Rapid access to data and information kept at a central place
- Central updating of information to ensure that it is of high quality
- Passage of memos via e-mail
- Sharing of common resources such as printers
- Documents to be easily transferred from user to user

6.5 INTERNET

The most popular for information superhighway is internet. The internet allows the individuals, businesses, universities and governments to interact with one another. The Internet enables communication between billions of connected computers across the world. Information is transmitted from client PCs whose users request services to server computers that hold information and host business applications deliver the services in response to requests.

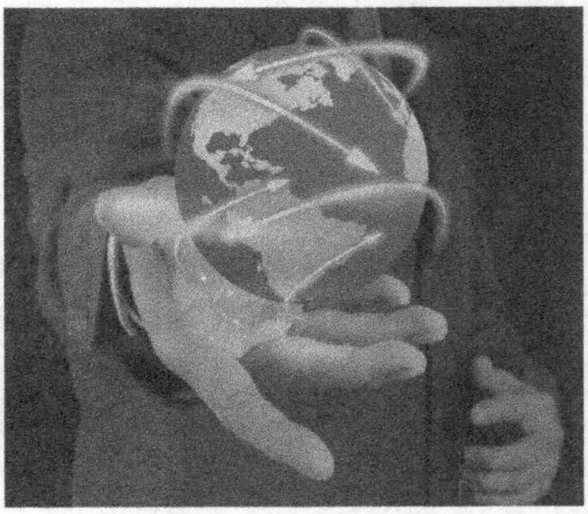

Internet services are constantly emerging. For example, a vast amount of information is available over the internet from libraries. The internet can provide critical information during times of disaster. The internet can also be used to translate words, sentences, or complete documents from one language into another.

The Internet has many advantages to organizations, which are as follows:

- Receives rapid access to information
- Can search for exactly the information needed
- Purchases can be made over the internet
- Easy to download material including software
- Rapid communication between a company and its customers.
- Huge savings on overheads, no warehouse space, etc.
- Good market research tool

6.6 E-MAILS

Electronic mail is currently the most common form of communication for both business and personal purposes. Electronic mail (e-mail) is the communication that takes place between computers. It requires a computer at the sender and receiver's ends, a modem and an internet connection. The advantage of using e-mail over other forms of communication is that organizations or individuals need not pay for each e-mail that they send or receive. Generally Electronic mail is defined as "a paperless written communication transmitted and received by computers".

6.6.1 Advantages of E-mails

E-mails allow organizations to send letters and files to another computer. There are many other advantages of e-mail for the organizations, which are as follows:

- It makes information more accessible.
- Provides faster and speedier communication in the organization.
- Quickest way of transmitting messages.
- Economical in the price.
- E-mails have contributed to the relationship building.
- One message can be sent to several people at the same time.

- Graphics and text can be easily sent with mail as an attachment.

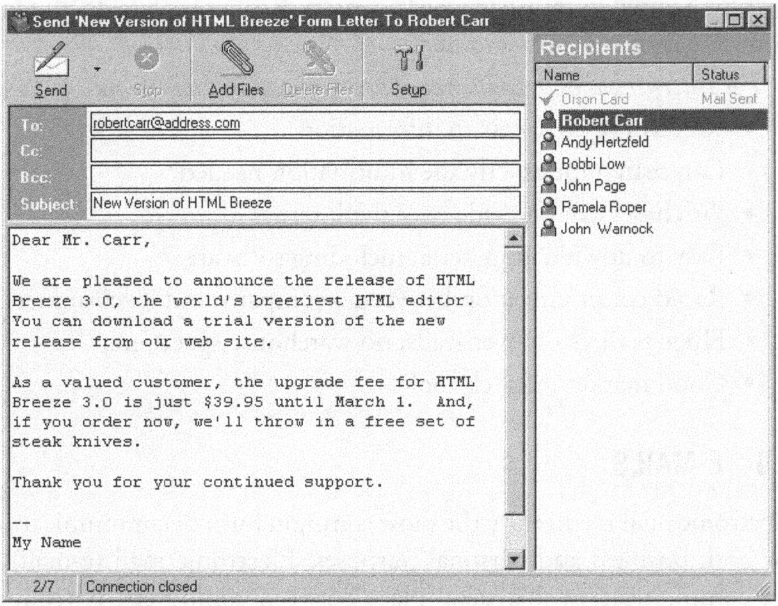

6.7 SHORT MESSAGE SERVICES (SMS)

The mobile or cellular telephone technology helps people to keep in touch with others whenever they want and irrespective of places wherever they may be. Modern cellular phones have various facilities, short message services (SMS), access to internet, voicemail, call waiting, conferencing are some examples.

SMS facilities became a very popular and inexpensive mode of communication in today's environment. These technologies are becoming important in our daily life. The mobile phones have made business more flexible. It has freed individuals or employees to confine in their offices and tables. For the people like share brokers and agents are always in touch with their clients at all times. It is possible to be in touch with the people who are in travel or out of their offices. Mobile phone usages are reducing the communication costs in very drastic way. Mobile technologies have many extra features that are found in new smart mobile phone like text messaging, memo, reminders, address book, personal organizer; web cam and Internet access. These technologies have reduced the distance and costs of the communication.

6.8 TELECONFERENCING

Communicating over telephones can be a cost effective substitute instead of face to face. It eliminates costly transit time and transportation expenses. It is estimated that teleconferencing are 75% less expensive than meeting in person. In teleconferencing all parties are connected via the telephone or audio conferencing. It is most productive and quite inexpensive. It is also called the "phone meeting". Conversation is possible with more than one person at the same time. Even teleconferencing connects people who are far apart and may be in different cities.

Source: howstuffworks.com

Basically three types of teleconferencing are found:

1. Audio teleconferencing
2. Audio graphic teleconferencing
3. Audio–videoconferencing.

Greater access, improved technology and reduced costs are making audio videoconferencing as their choice of medium, which is termed as videoconferencing.

6.9 VIDEOCONFERENCING

Videoconferencing allows people to hear and see each other at the same time in different locations. People can also speak to each other like having face-to-face discussions. With new technology, it is possible to connect more than two locations. It leads to more affordable conferencing if the members are scattered over the globe. In videoconferencing the discussions become more meaningful than interaction over the phone. Videoconferencing includes monitors, special cameras (web camera), speakers, codec, and equipment control pad at each location, digital microphones and network services to connect the locations.

Using Video-conferencing

The computer having a device called a codec converts all the analogue sound and pictures into digital signals. They are transmitted over digital telephone lines called ISDN (Integrated Services Digital Network) which need to have the necessary bandwidth to allow the transmission of digital signals.

Advantages of Videoconferencing are:

- Affordable conferencing, if team members are scattered
- Utmost like communicating face-to-face
- Employees or individuals remain available in the office
- Retention is better and more long lasting
- Enriches communication in many ways
- No need to travel to different location to conduct the meeting, so it avoids the stress
- Helps in reducing business related expenses like hotel bills or paying for the hire of conference conveniences.
- Can see the speaker, which is not possible with a telephone conference
- Documents can be shared and stored.

Case Study: How a Blog Aided a Nation

The Rotary Club of Colombo Regency in Sri Lanka invited a speaker to their club's meeting to teach members how to create a blog, not realizing how valuable this new technology would prove to be. Just one day after the world's deadliest tsunami destroyed parts of their country, the club members set up their first blog. It allowed people from all over the world to provide immediate assistance by donating money and providing food and medicine, and daily updates kept contributors informed about the club's relief efforts.

Club members e-mailed friends and family members to alert them to the blog and the account they had set up for donations. The club also made an arrangement with Lankafood.com— which did not benefit from the agreement — to take orders for food and medicine and send them directly to the Rotary Club of Colombo. Club members then purchased items from the local wholesale market and distributed them. Within a week, the club had raised nearly US$50,000 and an additional $35,000 had been pledged.

"Our club has been successful because we have been able to reach out the international community through this site," said club secretary Chamila Vickramasinghe.

Critical Thinking

Discuss the impact of technology based communication by considering the case study and how technological tools can be used for social purposes?

Summary

- Technology based communication tools has created a major insurrection in business practices. Technological developments have eliminated two great obstructions to communication- time and distance.
- Communications and information technology tools and software programs that aid the communication process from planning and developing to information gathering, analysing and organizing, writing and editing, presenting, storing, and distributing or sharing, technological tools can simplify and expedite the process.
- Technological tools can aid in preparing a written communication, such as letter, memo, or report, an oral presentation or any other type of communication project whether we are working on an individual project or group project.
- When we communicate with those above us, below us, or around us, we are establishing "Communication Networks". These may be formal channels or informal channels.
- Within the organization, there are four types of networks which are Wheel Chain, Circle and Star network
- Organizations use information and communication technology to coordinate their worldwide network of suppliers, distributors and consumers. Organizations have developed global information system that can track orders, their delivery status and payments at any time.

- Technological advances not only being new and better tools to the workplace but also increase the speed, frequency, and reach of communication. Advances in technology make it possible for more and more people to work away from the office-in cars, airports, hotels and even at home.
- Intranetware is an evolving concept which allows multi-users can have access to the same information and also called "Collaborative software".
- Intranetware includes document sharing and document management, group calendaring and scheduling, group contact and task management, threaded discussions, text chat, data conferencing and audio and video-conferencing.
- Intranets can also be used to provide access to all employees to get a copy of minutes of meeting, important presentations that might be reprocessed by different sales people, and information on the current status of manufacturing operations and so on.
- The internet allows the individuals, businesses, universities and governments to interact with one another. The internet enables communication between billions of connected computers across the world.
- The Internet can also be used to translate words, sentences, or complete documents from one language into another.
- Electronic mail (e-mail) is the communication that takes place between computers and also defined as "a paperless written communication transmitted and received by computers".
- SMS facilities became a very popular and inexpensive mode of communication in today's environment. Mobile technologies have many extra features that are found in new smart mobile phone like text messaging, memo, reminders, address book, personal organizer; Web cam and internet access.
- In teleconferencing all parties are connected via the telephone or audio conferencing. It is most productive and quite inexpensive. It is also called the "phone meeting".
- Three types of teleconferencing are found: Audio teleconferencing, Audio graphic teleconferencing and Audio- video conferencing.
- Video-conferencing allows people to hear and see each other at the same

time in different locations. People can also speak to each other like having face-to-face discussions.

- In video-conferencing, it is possible to connect more than two locations. It leads to more affordable conferencing if the members are scattered over the globe.

Exercises

1. What do you understand by communication network? Discuss the types of communication network found in the organizations.
2. Discuss the impact of technological advancement in organizational communication.
3. What is intranet and its advantages to the organizational communication?
4. Discuss the advantages of internet to the organizations.
5. Describe e-mail and its advantages.
6. What is teleconferencing? Also mention the types of teleconferencing.
7. Discuss about video-conferencing technology and related advantages.

Self-Check Questions

1. Technological developments have eliminated great obstructions to communication, which is
   (A) Time (B) Distance
   (C) Labor (D) A and B only
   (E) None of the above
2. A _______ network exists when there is a supervisor with a number of subordinates reporting directly without consultation or links with each other.
   (A) Wheel (B) Chain
   (C) Circle (D) Star
   (E) None of the above
3. _____________ allows multi-users can have access to the same information.
   (A) Internet (B) Intranet

(C) Electronic mail (D) SMS
(E) None of the above

4. All are the advantages of internet, Except:
   (A) Receives rapid access to information
   (B) Can search for exactly the information needed
   (C) Easy to download material including software
   (D) Good market research tool.
   (E) None of the above
5. The computer device which converts all the analogue sound and pictures into digital signals is known as
   (A) Digital microphones (B) Monitors
   (C) Codec (D) Web camera
   (E) None of the above

Answers

1. D 2. A 3. B 4. E 5. C

Part II

Media of Communication

7. Media of Communication
8. Speech
9. Telephoning Versus Face-To-Face Communication
10. Active Listening
11. Interview
12. Meeting
13. Business Letters
14. Business Reports

CHAPTER 7

Media of Communication

Contents of the Chapter

- The Basic Forms (Media) of Communication
- Non Verbal Communication
- Types of Non Verbal Communication
- Verbal Communication
- Oral Communication Media
- Written Communication Media

Learning Objectives

After finishing this chapter, students should be able to:

- The basic forms of communication and select the best form of communication for your message
- Differentiate between verbal and non-verbal communication
- Have understanding of situations to use each of the media types
- Recognize the importance of media in business communication
- Explain the advantages and disadvantages of oral communication
- Explain the advantages and disadvantages of written communication

7.1 INTRODUCTION

Media of communication is the channel through which messages are directed towards the receiver. Medium is the method used to deliver a message. As a business communicator, we can often choose whether to put our message in writing as a letter or memo. We can deliver our messages by hand or send it via regular mail or use delivery services like fax or electronic mail. Or we can communicate it orally, either over the phone or in person. We might also opt for non-verbal form of communication.

Whether we are a leader or a participant in a certain discussion or decision, we may use both written and oral means of communication. Frequently a request for action will be written, and then followed by an oral discussion of the proposal. Persuasion of either the reader or the listener is a central purpose in these media.

Communication with governmental departments and other agencies is mostly conducted through written letters. We can approach general public through advertisement on the radio, television, cinema screen, newspapers and popular journals. For communication to be effective the communicator has to be careful in opting of media, which will depend upon various factors like:

- Urgency of the message
- The time available
- The cost involved
- The intellectual and emotional level of the receiver
- Accessibility of media by the receiver.
- Educational background of the receiver, etc.

7.2 THE BASIC FORMS (MEDIA) OF COMMUNICATION

Communication occurs in many forms. We can pick up the phone and have a conversation with our supervisor or leave him e-mail message if he is not available. In turn, he can respond to our message in the form of his choice. The form in which a message is communicated changes constantly. There are various media through which we can send our message. They are generally divided into two:

Non-Verbal Communication

Nonverbal communication consists of that part of a message that is not encoded in words. The nonverbal part of the message often tends to reveal the sender's feelings and preferences more spontaneously and honestly than the verbal part. (*Sending message through media which does not use words-facial expression, gesture, other body movements*).

Verbal Communication

Verbal communication is communication through words either written or spoken. In this form, words are arranged according to the proper grammar rules and put in proper sequence as per the part of the speech. Examples of the verbal communication are a letter, memo, thank-you note, speech, and casual conversation.

Verbal communication is again divided into two categories:

Oral Media: Oral communication occurs in the situations like conversations, telephonic talks, interviews, presentations and meetings. Conferences, group discussions and speeches also form part of oral communication. (Communicating a message orally either over the phone or in person).

Written Media: Written communication includes letters, circulars, notices, memo, reports, forms, manuals. Everything that is put down on paper by writing comes under the purview of written communication. (Putting a message in writing as a letter, memo or any report) or using electronic devices such as electronic mail.

7.3 NON VERBAL COMMUNICATION

Non verbal communication is all intentional and unintentional messages that are neither written nor spoken. This type of communication sometimes referred as body language. It is expressed in term of body movements such as all the cues, gestures, facial expressions, spatial relationships, and attitude toward time that enable people to communicate without words.

Anthropologists theorize that long before human beings used words to talk things over, our ancestors communicated with one an other by using their bodies. They gritted their teeth to show anger; they smiled and touched one another to indicate affection. Although we have come a long way since those primitive times, we still use non-verbal cues to express superiority, dependence, dislike, respect, love and other feelings.

Non verbal communication differs from verbal communication in fundamental ways. For one thing, it is less structured, so it is more difficult to study. Even experts do not really know how people learn non-verbal behaviour. No one teaches a baby to cry or smile, yet these forms of self–expression are almost universal. Other types of nonverbal communication, such as the meaning of colours and certain gestures, vary from culture to culture.

Non verbal communication also differs from verbal communication in terms of intent and spontaneity. When we use verbal communication, we plan our words. We have a conscious purpose; we think about the message, if only for a moment. However, when we communicate nonverbally, we sometimes do so unconsciously.

7.4 MAIN FUNCTIONS OF NON VERBAL COMMUNICATION

Non-verbal communication plays an important role in any communication situation. It often plays a supplementary role to the verbal content delivered orally. Some other times, nonverbal symbols communicate on their own. More specifically, nonverbal communication serves the following functions:

- Substituting verbal messages
- Complementing the spoken words
- Regulating or accenting verbal message
- Expressing emotions and interpersonal attitudes
- Conveying personal/social/cultural identity

7.5 TYPES OF NON VERBAL COMMUNICATION

Everything from the simple shrug of the shoulder, the V-sign, the OK ring, the thumbs up gesture, eye movements, facial expressions, body postures, gestures, gait, clothing to the tone of voice, the accent. Non verbal components of communication also involve the use of space, of touch and smell and paralanguage. The types of non-verbal communication are almost limitless. However, in this part, we will cover only those types of non verbal communication which are most applicable to business communication:

- Facial expressions and eye contact
- Other Body movements and gestures
- Clothing and personal appearance
- Distance and personal space
- Physical environment
- Time

7.5.1 Facial Expressions and Eye Contact

Faces, it is said, is the mirror of the mind. The eyes and face are especially helpful means of communicating non verbally. They can express hidden emotions – *anger, annoyance, confusion, enthusiasm, fear, hatred, joy, love, interest, sorrow, surprise, uncertainty and others.* Our faces reveal how we are feeling inside while we might be trying to present a different emotion.

Eye contact is another important facet of eye behavior. This is because one can communicate a lot just with the help of the eyes. From *winking, seeing, glaring, staring eyes* can perform many functions.

For example: while telling a lie, a child tries to cover his or her mouth with both the hands. A teenager tries to cover her mouth with one hand. These gestures are called the 'mouth guard' gestures. Regarding eye contact a simple glare may stop students from talking, while a warm glance and an encouraging smile often win many friends.

Facial Expression & other emotional states

7.5.2 Other Body Movements and Gestures

Movements and gestures of other parts of the body are more closely tied to culture than facial expressions and eye contact. Ray Birdwhistell, an expert in the field of nonverbal communication, coined the term '*kinesics*" for the different body expressions. '*Kinesics*' means study of body movements.

Body movements and gestures may be given specific meaning by others regardless of your intentions.

For example: poor posture during an interview may be interpreted as disrespect, lack of enthusiasm, or indicative of poor work habits. The way a person stands may indicate self confidence, status, friendliness, and mood and so on. Even weak or overly strong hand shakes will be given some significance by many people.

As a business or professional person, we can improve our communication techniques by monitoring our conscious and unconscious body movements and gestures.

7.5.3 Clothing and Personal Appearance

Clothing and personal appearance also communicate non verbal messages. Our appearance and clothing help others determine our status, credibility and persuasiveness. Clothing, jewellery, hairstyles, cosmetics, fingernails, neatness, stature are part of personal appearance. They can convey impressions regarding occupation, age, sex, nationality, social and economic level, job status, and good or poor judgment, depending on circumstances. If your goal is to make a good impression, adopt the style of the people you want to impress. Clothes are means of decoration and self-expression. Clothing also indicates about a person's confidence, character and sociability. These are the reasons why it is said that '*clothes make a person*'.

7.5.4 Distance and Personal Space

The informal distance rules for conversing in various situations differ from culture to culture, family to family, and person to person. When others violate an individual's personal space requirements, that person becomes uncomfortable and will move to correct the distance. This is an addition way of communicating by use of 'space'. Often we place ourselves in certain special relationships with other people and objects. The study of these special factors is called '*proxemics*'.

Intimate distance ranges from actual contact to about 18 inches. We allow only intimate persons within this range. Of course, there is forced closeness as in the case of a crowded lift. Social distance is maintained with people with whom we are meeting for the first time. This distance ranges from 4feet to 12 feet. Many people are completely unaware of their personal distance requirements because, as we mentioned earlier, such requirements usually fall into the informal level of culture.

For example: In Ethiopia some of us unknowingly or knowingly hug a person we don't know with out worrying about his or her distance requirement. Research has shown that Australians speaking to acquaintances or work colleagues leave about an arm's length of space between themselves and the other person. People speaking to friends and family leave about half an arm or an elbow's length between themselves and others. People in intimate relationships allow direct and close contact when speaking to each other. The use of space reflects the way people feel about others.

7.5.5 Physical Environment

Psychologists state that each person reacts emotionally to the environment with "approach" (positive) or "avoidance" (negative) behaviour. Various researches have found that when participants perform tasks in "ugly" rooms, they experience "monotony, fatigue, headache, discontent, sleep, irritability, and unfriendliness". However, when performing tasks in "attractive" rooms, participants experience "feelings of pleasure, comfort, enjoyment, energy and desire to continue the activity."

7.5.6 Time

The way individuals use their time also communicates nonverbally. Arriving late for an appointment may diminish the importance that the visitor is perceived to attach to the appointment. Making someone wait for a scheduled appointment can also be interpreted to mean that the visitor is not very important to the person with whom he/she has the appointment. Cultures vary widely in the way they interpret the meaning attached to the use of time. Americans believe in arriving on time for an appointment. People of some other cultures are not affected by a visitor who arrives an hour late for an appointment. Whether it is acceptable to arrive late for an appointment often depends on whether you are meeting with someone of equal rank, some one more important, or some one less important. Also, anyone who is consistently late for appointments or in completing work assignments is often deemed inconsiderable or even undependable.

7.6 VERBAL COMMUNICATION

Verbal Communication consists of words arranged in meaningful patterns. Verbal communication can further be divided into two categories oral communication and written communication.

7.7 ORAL COMMUNICATION MEDIA

Oral communication media include face-to-face conversation (the richest medium), telephone calls, interviews, group discussion, conferences, announcements, speeches, presentations and meetings. Our choice between a face-to-face conversation and a telephone or video conference call would depend on audience location, message importance, and your need for the sort of nonverbal feedback, the only body language can reveal.

Advantages of Oral Communication

The main advantages of oral communication are as follows:

1. Provides for Immediate Feed Back

The speaker can get immediate feedback and clarify the ambiguity in oral communication particularly if it is face to face communication.

2. Saves Time

In case where action is required immediately, it is better to transmit the message orally.

3. Less Expensive

Oral communication saves money and other resources in comparison of other written communication

4. Effectiveness

In oral communication speaker can convey the message with the variation of tone, pitch and the intensity of the voice. It contributes to the effectiveness of the message.

5. Promotes Relationships

In the informal groups oral communication helps to promote the friendly relationships between the parties.

Disadvantages of Oral Communication

1. Oral communication is not possible if the communicator is far from each other and there is no mechanical device to connect them.
2. Oral communication is not suitable for lengthy messages, because there are chances to miss the important information.
3. Oral messages do not have any legal validity unless they are taped and made part of permanent records.

4. Oral messages can not be retained for a long time and also there is no record of transaction.
5. In oral communication responsibilities for mistakes, if any can not be specifically assigned.

7.8 WRITTEN COMMUNICATION MEDIA

Written messages also take many forms. They might be informal like the notes you use to exercise your own memories or formal like elaborate reports you submit to your supervisor. Written communication has one advantage. They let us plan and control the message.

A written format is appropriate when the information is complex, when a permanent record is needed for future reference, when the audience is large and geographically dispersed, and when immediate interaction with the audience is either unimportant or undesirable.

This category includes letters, memos, telegrams, and minutes of meetings, proposals, forms, questionnaire and reports. Most letters and memos are relatively brief documents, generally one to two pages. Memos are the work horses of business communication, used for the routine, day–to–day exchange of information within the organization. The use memo is to designate responsibility, communicate the same material to many people, communicate policy and procedure, confirm oral agreements or decisions, and place specific information on record. In contrast, letters frequently go to outsiders, and they perform an important public relations function in addition to conveying a particular message.

Letters and memos are organized according to their purpose; the relationship between writer and reader dictates their style and tone.

Reports and proposals are factual, objective documents that may be distributed to either insiders or outsiders, depending on their purpose and subject. Reports are generally longer and more formal than letters and memos, and they have more components. Generally, written communication increases the sender's control but eliminates the possibility of immediate feedback.

Use Written Communication when:

- The sender wants a record for future references.
- The receiver will be referring to it later.
- The message is complex and requires study by the receiver.
- The message includes a step by step procedure.
- Oral communication is not possible because people are not in the same place at the same time.
- There are many receivers. Caution: the receivers must be interested in the subject and will put forth the time and effort to read and understand.
- A copy of the message should go to another person.
- The receiver prefers written.

Advantages of the Written Communication

The main advantages of written communication are as follows:

1. Permanent Record

Written communication becomes permanent record for the organization and can be very useful for the future reference. Old order and decisions can help us to take new decisions, formulating new policies and fixing current targets.

2. Legal Document

Written communication is accepted as a legal document; normally executives take every action in written form instead of making it orally.

3. Accurate and Precise

Written communication is usually developed with care. Executives are very much conscious while writing and give a serious thought to his ideas and organize the message very carefully. It is more appropriate for lengthy messages.

4. Wide Access

Written communication has a wide access. Written communication can be sent through post or mail, if sender and receiver are at different places. It proves the cheaper cost of communication between them.

5. Documented and used as a Reference

In the written communication the receiver can go through the message again and again, until he/she properly understands the message. In oral communication important information may be missed or misunderstood. In written communication such type of possibilities are minimized. It provides a permanent record for future reference, which may be used as a proof of evidence.

Disadvantages of Written Communication

1. Expensive in Terms of Time and Money

The major limitation in written communication is that it is time consuming. In oral communication messages can be transmitted through telephone and we can get response immediately, but in written communication a letter may take couple of weeks to reach its destination. Written communication is costly in terms of different resources. It is not only postage expense but also a number of human resource and other resources.

2. Less Flexible

Written media of communication does not provide flexibility because frequent changes of message leads to loss of credibility. Moreover, it does not provide a chance to use non verbal communication.

3. Immediate Response is Not Possible

In case of written communication if receiver has certain doubt he can not get the immediate clarification, which is possible in oral communication. In such case receiver has to write back and wait until the reply comes.

Summary

- Medium is the method used to send message. There are various media through which you can send your message. They are generally divided into three: Oral media (communicating a message orally either over the phone or in person), written media (putting a message in writing as a letter, memo or any report) or using electronic devices such as electronic mail or fax), and non-verbal media (sending message through media which does not use words-facial expression, gesture, other body movements).
- Verbal communication uses words arranged in meaningful patterns. The two major types of verbal communication are oral and written communication.
- Oral communication consists of face-to-face conversation, telephone calls, speeches, presentations and meeting. Their choice depends on audience location and message importance.
- The advantages of oral communication are that it provides immediate feedback, saves time, less expensive, effective and promotes feedback. The limitations of oral communication are that it is not suitable for lengthy messages and have no legal proof of it.
- Written messages might take formal or informal forms. The most common types of written communication media are letters, memos and reports.
- Non-verbal communication is all intentional or unintentional messages that are neither written nor spoken. Non-verbal communication media include gestures, facial expressions, spatial relationships and attitudes toward time.

Exercises

- What is media of communication? Explain.
- What is non-verbal communication?
- Explain the types of non-verbal communication applicable in business communication.
- What is oral communication?
- Explain the advantages and disadvantages of oral communication.
- What is written communication media?
- Mention the advantages and disadvantages of written communication.

Self-Check Questions

1. Which of the following is not a medium through which a message is sent
   (A) Speech
   (B) Teleconference
   (C) Fax
   (D) Letter
   (E) None of the above
2. Which of the following is the most basic form of communication
   (A) Telephoning
   (B) Using body movements
   (C) Electronic mail
   (D) Memo
   (E) None of the above
3. An oral channel is the best under the following situations except
   (A) You do not need a permanent record
   (B) You want immediate feedback
   (C) You do need a permanent and verifiable record
   (D) Your message is relatively simple
   (E) None of the above
4. Which of the following statements does not characterize non-verbal communication?
   (A) Nonverbal communication is spontaneous and is difficult to plan
   (B) Nonverbal communication sometimes is made unconsciously out of your mind control
   (C) Nonverbal communication is structured
   (D) Nonverbal communication is difficult to learn and study
   (E) Nonverbal communications vary from culture to culture
5. Brief documents usually used for internal communication within an organization and also Coined as "work horses" are said to be
   (A) Letters
   (B) Memos
   (C) Proposals
   (D) Reports

Answers

1. E 2. B 3. C 4. C 5. B

CHAPTER 8

Speech

Contents of the Chapter

- Oral Presentations
- Types of Speech
- Parts of Speech
- Modes of Speech Delivery
- Characteristics of Good Speaker
- Guidelines for an Effective Delivery of Speech

Learning Objectives

After finishing this chapter, students should be able to:

- Define Speech
- Define Presentations
- Prepare short & long presentations
- Identify the different types of speech
- Describe the importance of speech
- Understand the characteristics of a good speaker
- Identify the different parts of speech
- Understand the general guidelines for an effective delivery of speech

8.1 INTRODUCTION

Speech is the process to create a common understanding among people within a business environment by means of spoken language. The widely applied means of oral communication in face-to-face business situations are listening short talks and presentations, conducting interview and meetings. Speech is one of the media of communication that we use to deliver message or information for many people at once.

In the world of business, managers communicate with their customers, colleagues, associates, superiors, employees, employers and others. But this communication does not need any special preparation as this is simply a face to face conversation in which managers can convey their message very easily and without any hesitation. However, at certain occasion managers have to talk to a big audience such as employees to convince then to do hard work and customers to trust you.

A key rule to make a good speech is to keep in mind that audiences care most about things that directly affect them. An effective speaker understands the nature of audiences and adapts speeches to audiences. In order to do this, we must learn everything about our particular audience. Then make sure to keep the audience in mind in every decision we make in the speech development process. When we plan our speech this way, we engage in "audience-centered" approach, which is vital for success.

8.2 ORAL PRESENTATIONS

"This is the action of communication in which one speaker is doing most of the sending and a number of listeners are doing most of the receiving it is known as oral presentation."

During the business career, it will be required to make a variety of oral presentations. These may be as short as five minutes, such as for introducing a speaker, or as long as one hour, such as for making a technical presentation. The size of the audience may vary from one individual to hundreds, and the purpose may vary from informative to comparative to persuasive.

8.2.1 The Short Presentation

Like written communications, speeches must be well planned. Analyze your audience and note how much time is allotted to you to speak. Planning your talk in relationship with your allotted time and with audience level is very important. However, the critical factor in planning is the organization of the presentation itself. The communicator must carefully determine the major topics and minor areas, then integrate them in a logical order for the greatest impact on the audience.

Choose Your Approach

With a well-defined idea you begin to arrange your message

- Structure a short oral presentation like a letter or a memo
- Organize language speeches and presentations like formal reports.
- For persuasive plan to arouse interest, give a preview to audience.

8.2.2 The Long Presentation

Sometimes you will be asked to present a rather lengthy speech to inform members of an audience of new policies, procedures, or products; to exchange technical material; to present research findings; or to analyze budget considerations. *The long presentation differs from the short one in several ways: The length of the long presentation may vary from 10 to 60 minutes, Visuals are used more frequently in the long presentation, the concepts and ideas in the long presentation are usually more complex, and audience involvement and participation are more common in the long presentation.*

Choose Your Approach

- If purpose is to entertain, motivate or inform, use direct order and a structure imposed naturally by the subject. Importance, sequence, chronology, spatial orientation, geography or category.
- If your purpose is to analyze, persuade or collaborate, organize your material around conclusions and recommendations or around a logical arguments.

- Use direct order if the audience is receptive, use indirect if you expect resistance.

Regardless of the length of your presentation, bear in mind that simplicity of organization is valuable in oral presentation.

8.3 TYPES OF SPEECH

Although there are many different types of oral presentations, they can be divided into three general categories; *Presentation to inform, persuade and to entertain.* Since entertainment is rarely the purpose of speeches by entry level employees and supervisors, we will discuss only informative and persuasive presentations.

8.3.1 Informative Presentations

Informative presentations occur continually in business and professional organizations. Although there is some overlap between informative and persuasive presentations, informative presentations are intended to increase understanding, not to change an attitude. The majority of informative presentations are informal in nature, most employees are expected to organize and present informal briefings and reports to colleagues and supervisors as a normal part of their jobs.

Types of Informative Presentations

The basic purpose of an informative presentation is to promote understanding of ideas. Many types of informative presentation are used in business situation. Although, the names given of various informative presentations differ greatly from company to company here we will discuss some of them. Examples of informative presentations are:

- Oral briefing
- Oral report
- Instructions
- Community good will

Oral Briefing: Oral briefing is designed to present a summary of facts in a short period of time (usually fifteen minutes or less). A briefing may be given to an individual (such as an employee, supervisor, or client). Many briefings are informal; when an employee or supervisor informally presents information to colleagues at a weekly meeting. Other briefings are more formal, such as a briefing on the status of a particular project given to an entire department. Since briefings last only a short time, few visuals are required.

It is impossible for supervisors to observe all events or situations themselves. Consequently, informative briefings and reports presented by their employees are the only way supervisors can stay up to date on the incredible amount of information they need to make sound decisions.

Oral Report: Oral report is designed to present complete details and requires a longer period of time (usually more than fifteen minutes). A report may be a research report on the feasibility of producing a new item, an analytical report examining various ingredients such as those used to strengthen a type of plastic, a demonstrative report explaining how to use a new machine or company product, or an investigative report examining a problem area. Often decision making groups are required to prepare both written and oral reports on a problem and their recommendations for solving it. Like the briefings reports may be informal or formal but tend to be more formal than the most briefings.

If the report includes recommendations, the recommendations should be presented in an informative (not persuasive) manner and include both advantages and disadvantages. The detailed information presented in a report can be simplified by the use of visual aids.

Supervisors use briefings and reports to communicate company policies and operational procedures downward to employees. Employees use briefings and reports to:

1. Communicate ideas and proposals upward to supervisors and horizontally to fellow workers and
2. To present information or demonstrate product use to clients.

Instructions: This is aimed at making clear a process or policy or even the philosophy of a company mostly to newly coming employees. It requires listeners to follow the explanation, learn from the instructions and then apply it within the organization.

Community good will: These are made by organizations that realize the value of remaining in contact with the community. Sensitive organizations spend considerable time and money to support their public relation offices that are meant to look after and leave a positive company image in the minds of the community.

8.3.2 Persuasive Presentations

The basic purpose of a persuasive presentation is to influence choices. Persuasion (specifically, selling ideas) was listed earlier as one of the most often used communication skills by people in entry level jobs, it may very well be one of the least effectively used.

Business people view persuasion as intimidation. They feel that the only way to get people to do what they want is by force or trickery. Neither of these methods is effective and neither is really persuasion.

"*Persuasion is communication intended to influence choice*" but it is not the same as intimidation. To inform is to increase the number of person's options or choices (*the more you know, the more choices you have*). To persuade is to limit the options that are perceived as acceptable"

There is no force or trickery in persuasion. The receivers of the persuasive message must weigh the logic and evidence and make their own decision. Once that decision has been made, they alone are responsible for it, although the sender helped in influening the decision.

In business our ability to achieve the company's goals depends on our ability to persuade others.

8.4 PARTS OF SPEECH

Regardless of the job or the purpose of the presentation, Speech has three main parts:

1. Introduction
2. Body and
3. Conclusion

8.4.1 INTRODUCTION

Introduction is to take place at the first few minutes of our speech. The introduction of an oral presentation should:

1. Capture the attention of your listeners
2. Motivate them to listen by showing the importance or benefit your presentation will have for them
3. Convince them that you are qualified to speak on the subject, and
4. Explain the purpose of your presentation.

Capture the Attention of Your Listeners

As you begin your presentation, listeners' attention may be focused on many personal things. So in this introductory part you are expected to direct the attention from individual concerns and thoughts to your presentation. Same common techniques for gaining attention are:

- Reveal one or more starling facts.
- Tell joke or humorous story relating directly to the topic.
- Briefly cite two or three specific incidents or examples that relate to the topic.
- Quote or paraphrase a well-known publication or expert.
- Briefly demonstrate the item or skill you will be discussing in your presentation.

Convince the Audience of the Benefit to them

Capturing the initial attention of your listeners does not guarantee that they will listen to the remainder of your presentation. To keep their attention you must convince them that the presentation will benefit them in same way- that is, will help them satisfy personal or job-related needs.

Assure the Audience that you are Qualified to Speak on the Subject

The speaker is expected to demonstrate his qualification to speak on the topic by referring to his personal experience, the detailed research he has done on the topic, the interview he has conducted with knowledgeable people or the articles and books he has read that were written by experts. By doing so the speaker should have to convince the audiences as he has the knowledge on the topic.

Explain the Purpose of your Presentation

Here the speaker is expected to state the purpose and a summary of the main points to be covered. The average listener finds it much easier to follow and remember the ideas contained in the presentation when the introduction lists the key points that will be covered.

8.4.2 Body

In the main body of the speech the main points that are summarized in the introduction part needs to be discussed in detail. Most speakers cover, two, three or four main points in their presentation.

Researchers have found that people are "capable of accurately receiving and remembering only seven facts, ideas or "bits" of information at a time". Therefore, organize the information into seven or fewer key ideas or main points.

The number of main points that should be included depends on

1. How many points are needed to adequately develop the topic
2. The time limit
3. The knowledge and interest of the audience.

The main points can be organized in a variety of methods. The arrangements that seem to be most relevant to business and professional situations are:

Topical Arrangement

This arrangement is used to break a topic into clusters, divisions, or parts. No spatial, chronological, or casual relationship exists between the main points in a topical arrangement; each is merely one of several topics pertaining to the same subject. It is probably the easiest, and therefore, the most popular method of arrangement. It is most effective when arranged in one of the following ways:

- From the most to the least popular
- From the most to the least impressive
- From the known to the unknown
- From the familiar to the unfamiliar

Spatial or Geographical Arrangement

This arrangement organizes main points according to their spatial location, such as front to rear, north to south, bottom to top, left to right. The lay out of a manufacturing plant could be described by its left, centre and right wings.

Chronological or Time Arrangement

This arrangement is used to present events in the order (or by the date) of their occurrence and to present steps in the order in which they occur or in the order in which they should be followed.

Problem-Solution Arrangement

This arrangement divides the speech in to two basic categories:

The analysis of the problem and the explanation of one of several solutions.

8.4.3 The Conclusion

The conclusion normally contains two parts: a summary and a closing thought or statement. The summary can be general (referring to the overall topic of the presentation) or specific (listing the main points covered). The intent of the summary is to clarify for the listeners any contusions about the purpose and main points of your presentation.

The closing thought or statement serves as a final attention getter. Its purpose is to give the audience a thought or challenge that will keep them thinking about your presentation long after it is completed.

8.5 MODES OF SPEECH DELIVERY

There are four modes of delivery

8.5.1 Reading from a Manuscript

Reading from a manuscript is the most formal type of delivery. It is also an effective choice when we want to have the greatest control of the wording of our speech. We will probably use a manuscript when speaking on a highly sensitive topic for which it is important to have precise wording.

Reading from manuscript seriously limits the ability to:

1. *Exhibit a natural style,*
2. *Maintain eye contact,*
3. *Observe and evaluate feedback, and*
4. *Adjust the messages.*

Therefore, never use the written style just out of fear of facing an audience, of forgetting the material, or of encoding messages improperly. Overcome that fear through practice and experience.

8.5.2 Presenting from Memory

A memorized speech can also sound "canned" and lacking in spontaneity. Some speakers, however, are extremely skillful at memorizing. Others, who have presented the same ideas a number of times, will memorize their lines whether they intended to or not. Each time they speak on that or a similar topic, they can draw from memory. The imperfections exist in the memorized approach are:

1. *The difficulty of memorizing more than a few paragraphs,*
2. *The possibility of forgetting material during the speech, and*
3. *The difficulty in presenting a memorized speech in a no mechanical manner*

8.5.3 Speaking Extemporaneously

When we speak extemporaneously that does not mean that we do not do preparation. Rather, as we rehearse our work from an outline or speaker notes that remind us the progression of ideas in our speech. An extemporaneous speech is likely to be very dynamic and sound spontaneous and fresh.

Choose the extemporaneous style above all of the others. It has the advantages of preparation, naturalness, flexibility, spontaneity, and full interaction with the audience. To develop an extemporaneous speech:

- Develop the speech by first writing and revising an outline. Write only a few sentences – and perhaps the opening and the closing.
- Place the outline or key words and phrases, possibly all in capital letters, on only one side of note cards. Leave plenty of space around and between lines.
- Using the note cards only when necessary, practice speaking aloud several times before a videotape camera, friends, or a mirror to improve delivery, sentence construction, eye contact, etc.

- Avoid practicing to the point that you memorize a fixed pattern of words. Practice only you know that you will speak in a coherent but spontaneous manner.
- Apply all of the suggestions for good verbal and nonverbal presentations.

8.5.4 Impromptu Speech

The impromptu speech occurs with little or no time for preparation. The reduced chances for analyzing the audience, organizing, and encoding require a fast-thinking speaker. When delivering an impromptu speech, use these suggestions:

- *At even a hint that you may have to speak, begin to apply the guidelines, even while walking or turning to face the audience.*
- *Move the planning directly to the specific topic, objectives, and key points. Write them on paper if you have the seconds necessary to do so.*
- *When first facing the audience, take a few seconds to form the first words silently before speaking them.*
- *Watch for feedback to know when to repeat or clarify.*
- *Speak briefly, and conclude firmly.*
- *If appropriate, ask if the audience has questions.*

8.6 CHARACTERISTICS OF A GOOD SPEAKER

Every good speech requires careful preparation. The speaker must be ready to cover the subject thoroughly and must carefully organize the presentation. Here below are the guidelines of being a good speaker:

1. Know the subject
2. Know the audience
3. Be well organized

The oral presentation must be well organized logically starting from the planning process. If you have the following points, it will be easier:

1. Decide on the order that will be followed
2. Set down the basic ideas you want to express (and consider different ways of arranging them). Thus organize the information in a form of introduction, body and conclusion.
3. State what you want to discuss clearly (problem? process? project?)
4. Involve your listener
   (i) Tell a real story
   (ii) Tell a hypothetical story
   (iii) Present statistics
   (iv) Use of quotation
   (v) Tell a joke
5. Plan your conclusion

8.7 GUIDELINES FOR AN EFFECTIVE DELIVERY OF SPEECH

Speech is series of thoughts in the mind. There are about seven guidelines for speech:

- Look at your audience
- Speak clearly
- Use appropriate gestures
- Check your postures and appearance
- Make clear transition
- Vary your volume and speed
- Watch and listen for feedback

8.7.1 Look at Your Audience

The easiest way to do this is to look at the audience. This does not mean a periodical quick look at the group. Rather it means talking with them and looking at them. Do not look podium at the platform or over the heads. Be alert for the audience's feedback and make the necessary adjustment. Make good eye contact (it helps to build a link between you and the audience). All these will permit you to relate your information to them and not at them. Look at those in the middle section, then those to the right, and then those to the left. Let your eyes rest on different sections of the audience and a mass of faces. For the effectiveness of your delivery of speech you need to have a clear eye contact with your audience and you need to make sure that whether your audiences are following you or not.

8.7.2 Speak Clearly

The speech is related to accent. Accent is pronounced noticeably. Pronunciation means saying words correctly, while enunciation means saying words distinctly. Both are necessary if you are to be understood and wish to make a good impression on others. Your accent of words phrases and sentences needs to be in line with the accent of your audiences and it should be easily understandable.

8.7.3 Use Appropriate Gesture

Gesture adds to the message you communicate. Although, gestures have vague meanings, they are strong. They are natural aid to speaking. It should be clear that you could use bodily movements to help your speaking. Which movement you should use, however, is hard to say. They are related to personality, physical make up, and the size and the nature of the audience. A speaker appearing before a formal group generally should use relatively few body actions. A speaker appearing before an informal audience should use more what you should use on a given occasion is a matter for your best judgment. Your body movement while you are on presentation has a significant impact on the effective delivery of your speech so need to consider these things in your presentation.

8.7.4 Check your Posture and Appearance

Obviously, speaker will dress and stand in a manner appropriate for the presentation. Do not let your appearance, posture, or destructing gestures override your message. It is important for you to dress properly, stand correctly and bring the focus of the audience to your message and not to destructions, have others tell you whether your posture needs improvement. Another is to practice speaking before a mirror or with video type equipment. In your efforts to improve your posture, keep in mind what must go on with your body in order for good posture.

8.7.5 Make Clear Transition

It is possible to cover topics faster so that the audience may follow them properly. Therefore, it is vital that you watch your transitions. At the end of a major point, slow down or pause for a moment. Then, instead of abruptly starting the next idea, tell the audience that you are now moving from your expiations of 'communication goals' to communication skills. Statements like these are called transitions and they tell the audience to switch gears and prepare for the next item in the speech. Transitions provide a rest for listeners and also give a clear signal about where you were and where you are going now. Some common transitions that might be used are:

- 'Now let's turn to another point…'
- However, there is another aspect that we should look at today…..'
- 'Now with our understanding of…we can discuss …'

Thus, when the transition is stated slowly, you look at the audience and incorporate gesture with the transition. The audience will understand what is being said and will know what will be said.

8.7.6 Vary Your Volume and Speed

A boring speech may put your audience to sleep. Some ideas need to be started forcefully; others need to be noted softly respectfully. Look for a good piece that is fast, slow, high low loud or soft, so should a speech reflect changes that match with the content of the idea. A speech could be as boring and monotonous as a piece of music that proceeds at one volume level and speed only. As a general rule, you should present the easy parts of the message at a fairly quick rate and hard to understand information at a lower (slower pace). The reason for varying the speed of the presentation should be apparent. Easy information presented slowly is irritating, hard information presented rapidly may be difficult to understand. By observing your audiences condition in the presentation you should vary your volume and speed of voice to hold their attention.

8.7.7 Watch and Listen Feedback

You can and should train your self to watch the audience as you speak and to be sensitive to its changing moods. The alert speakes will be on the look out for a feed back. If the audience looks confused on a particular point you can assist by interjecting a statement like 'let me repeat that... or perhaps I can state this concept in another way ...' Besides helping the audience to understand the message, such statements indicate that the speaker is paying attention to the audience. Also if the audience laughs longer than expected at a humorous comment, the speaker pauses and permits the audience and to catch up. By looking at the people in the audience and interpreting their feedback, you can keep the message on target. Successful interaction with the audience is, to a large extent the element that makes your audiences glad for coming to hear you.

Thus, to deliver the speech, check your volume, keep your head up, use conversational tone, and hide your nervousness. Stand at ease, avoid mannerisms, use the time allotted. Observe audience reaction, carefully select the closing words. Conversational tone refers to the usage of simple language to the audience, where as mannerism is articulation of word not clearly and over usage of ah, uh etc.

TIPS

Making a Good Speech

- Keep your audience in mind
- Speak slowly, vigorously, and enthusiastically
- Use gestures to accentuate points
- Maintain eye contact with your audience
- Rehearse your presentation until you are comfortable.
- If possible, record your speech. Listen to what you have said as objectively as possible
- If possible, become familiar with the room
- Try not to provide the audience hand-out material before you begin.

Overcoming Stage Distress

- Know the room
- Know the audience
- Know your material
- Relax
- Visualize yourself giving your speech
- Realize that people want you to succeed
- Don't apologize
- Turn nervousness into positive energy
- Gain experience

Summary

- Speech is the process of establishing a common understanding among people within a business environment by means of spoken language
- There are three types of oral presentation: presentation to inform, persuade and to entertain.
- Informative presentations are intended to increase understanding, not to change an attitude while the basic purpose of a persuasive presentation is to influence choices.
- There are four modes of speech Delivery, which are Reading from a manuscript, Presenting from memory, Speaking Extemporaneously, Impromptu speech.
- Speech has three main parts: Introduction, Body and Conclusion. The introduction part intends to capture the attention of your listeners, convince the audience of the benefit to them, assure the audience that you are qualified to speak on the subject, and explain the purpose of your presentation. In the main body of the speech the main points that are summarized in the introduction part need to be discussed in detail. The conclusion normally contains a summary and a closing thought or statement.
- A good speaker knows the subject and the audience, and is well organized. The guidelines for effective delivery of speech are: Look at your audience, Speak clearly, Use appropriate gestures, Check your postures and appearance, Make clear transition, Vary your volume and speed, and Watch and listen for feedback.

Exercises

1. What is a speech? Explain.
2. Explain the purpose of informative presentations.
3. Explain the types of informative presentations.
4. What is a persuasive presentation?
5. Explain briefly the parts of speech.
6. Mention the characteristics of a good speaker.
7. Explain the guidelines for an effective delivery of speech.

Self-Check Questions

1. If a person writes down a speech in such a way that the material to be presented is put in the order in which it took place this can be considered as
   (A) General organization (B) Cause to effect
   (C) Chronological organization (D) None of the above
2. From which part of speech the detailed idea of the speech can be best obtained
   (A) Conclusion (B) Body
   (C) Introduction (D) All
   (E) None of the above
3. Which one is different from others?
   (A) Look at your audience (B) Vary your volume and speed
   (C) Speak clearly (D) Make clear transition
   (E) None of the above
4. The arrangement used to present events in the order of their occurrence is
   (A) Problem solution arrangement
   (B) Chronological arrangement
   (C) Spatial or geographical arrangement
   (D) Topical arrangement
   (E) None

Fill the blank space with appropriate terms

5. ____________ contains two parts, a summary and a closing thought or statement
6. ____________is aimed at making clear a process or policy or even philosophy of a company mostly to younger employees.
7. The main idea of a speech is found in __________________ part.
8. ___________ is designed to present complete details and requires a short period of time.
9. The basic purpose of ___________________ is to influence choices.

Answers

1. C
2. B
3. E
4. B
5. Conclusion
6. Instruction
7. Body
8. Oral report
9. Persuasion

CHAPTER 9

Telephoning Versus Face-to-Face Communication

Contents of the Chapter

Learning Objectives

After finishing this chapter, students should be able to:

- Identify characteristics of face-to-face conversation and telephoning
- Understand the checklists for effective face-to-face communication
- Identify and understand the procedures to be followed by the caller and the receiver before and during telephoning
- Describe the merits and demerits of face-to-face conversation and telephoning
- Understand the importance of face-to-face and telephone conversation for business organizations

9.1 INTRODUCTION

Oral communication is the life – blood of our personal and business lives. Our ability to communicate is a process which begins in childhood; the roles we play become gradually more complex as we become adults and assume more responsibility. The essential ingredient is you, and it is important in this respect to recognize that you play two roles in oral communication: listening as well as speaking.

If we aim at a success of our secretarial career, and whatever career may follow, our success will depend on much more than our practical skills no matter how good our short hand or typing skills or our ability to present documents effectively, we will not get for if we can not get along with people.

9.2 CHARACTERISTICS OF FACE-TO-FACE CONVERSATION

In business life we will probably spend much more of our time talking and listening to colleagues and clients than writing and listening to colleagues and clients. Problems will need to be discussed, information requested, instructions given. We spend much of our lives speaking to other people, but something strange happens to many of us when we are asked to speak in front of a group or in a formalized situation. To achieve co-operation and effective teamwork, good human relations skills must be developed.

Face-to-face Communication can take a variety of forms

- Private discussion
- A conversation over lunch
- A gossip in the lift
- A chance meeting in the corridor
- An informal gathering of staff
- Instructing subordinates
- Dealing with clients
- Formal meetings
- Interviews/ seminars

In face-to-face communication, we have various means of conveying information: modulation of the voice, facial expressions, gesture, posture and movement. These factors add impact to a meaning, and they combine to provide an instant impression in a way that written communication or telephone calls cannot.

The following are characteristics of face-to-face communication:

- It takes different forms like private discussion, formal meetings, dealing with clients and so on
- It requires two groups, the speaker and the listener
- It is natural for the parties involved in it
- It is supported by non verbal cues to convey information like intonation of voice, facial expression, gesture, posture and body movement
- It is supplemented by verbal language
- It provides immediate feedback
- It needs no charge for conversation
- More reliable and effective

9.3 CHECKLISTS FOR EFFECTIVE FACE-TO-FACE COMMUNICATION

1. Plan what you will say-prepare supporting notes and gather any relevant documents.
2. Consider the person to whom you will be speaking, take account of their position, background, knowledge and experience
3. Speak appropriately to the situation – Be chatty, friendly, informal or formal, etc, in accordance with the situation and the topic.
4. Be open – minded consider the matter from the other person's point of view and be as open minded as possible, but have counter – arguments ready just in case they are required.
5. Consider the location – you will feel more comfortable in a familiar environment. Try to avoid distractions like telephone calls or other interruptions.

9.4 MERITS AND DEMERITS OF FACE-TO-FACE CONVERSATION

Merit	Demerit
Supplemented by verbal language	Inaccuracy due to non-permanent record
Natural for communicators	Less concise
It needs no charge for the conversation	It depends on the location of communicators
More reliable and effective	Immediate response may lead communicators to unconscious action
It enables more people to participate at once	Unwise use of both verbal and non-verbal language may be the cause for quarrel
It avoids misunderstanding when two communicators talk uses non verbal language like facial expression etc face-to-face	In face-to-face communication the communicator may be influenced by external environment i.e. status, physical appearance etc

9.5 TELEPHONE CONVERSATION

Ever since Graham Bell made it possible for people at away places to get connected, the telephone has been an essential tool for business and social communication. The telephone is a channel that a modern manager cannot do without.

It is a form of instant communication which achieves quick responses, but it takes imagination to use a telephone effectively. As we cannot see the other person or know that he/she is thinking, our communication will be only as effective as our words and the way they are used, for example intonation, style of delivery. It is ear –to – ear communication which means that it doesn't allow the use of body language unlike that of face–to–face communication.

In any organization, the person on the telephone represents the company. That person gives an impression of the company to the outside world; whether making or receiving the call. There can be nothing more damaging for public relations, or better for losing business than a telephone call which leaves the caller frustrated and no better informed than before he or she started. The impression any organization wishes to convey to the outside world is of an efficient, friendly, progressive company eager to give product and service and ensure good public relations.

It is a very useful channel for quick local, national, and international communication. But it has a severe limitation – communicators and communicatees have to depend exclusively on voice. The total absence of visual and near–total absence of other non-verbal support (except notably for tone of voice) makes it imperative that we follow certain guidelines when we use the telephone channel for one – to – one calls or conference calls.

9.6 CHARACTERISTICS OF TELEPHONE CONVERSATION

- It requires electronic device-telephone
- It requires two people to involve – the caller and the receiver
- It is persuasive
- It gives immediate feedback
- It needs charge for conversation

- Overcomes the limitation of distance
- Sharing of information with in a very short period of time
- Facilitates information exchange

Procedures to be Followed by the Caller and the Reciever

As well other successful written and oral communication, telephoning requires preplanning by the caller and desirable behaviour during the conversation by both persons who are conversing. As some commercial advices "Reach out and touch some one". Though you are not meeting face-to-face, your conversation will be voice-to-voice and you want it to be as favourable as possible.

Before Telephoning

1. Know the specific purpose of your call
2. Know the name and occupation (if pertinent) of the person you are calling
3. Consider the best time to call, from the stand point of that person and your company. Usually, avoid calling just before lunch or at closing time. If you are calling long distance, be sure to consider time zones, consult your phone director map choose discount times whenever possible and desirable.
4. Plan your opening statement
5. Jot down the questions you want to ask try to limit your call to one main point. If you are calling to sell something, know your sales psychology and have factual suggestions for listener benefits
6. Have paper and pen handy for note – taking, taking telephone messages require both oral and written communication skills. A pencil and telephone message pad should be kept by the telephone. The message pad provides headings which act as a reminder to obtain the necessary information from the caller.

During Telephoning

- Introduce your self.
- Announce your name the organization and greet the caller.
- Be polite avoid a barking tone.

- When you answer a phone call with clear pleasant voice answer promptly, usually with your name/ department/ organization and greet the caller.
- If the person you are calling is not there you can leave a message with your number and time to have your call returned.

- If the call is to be directed, make sure the caller is not made to wait on the line for long.
- If the person called is not available, make a note of the caller's name, telephone number and message and communicate to the person concerned.
- Keep personal talk on the official line to the minimum.
- Calls cost money; especially long distance ones make your talk cost – effective.
- Make sure that the calls are returned promptly.
- End the conversation with a "thank you" or a good day".

9.7 MERITS AND DEMERITS OF TELEPHONE CONVERSATION

Merits	Demerits
Sharing of ideas easily in a short period of time	It cannot be supplemented by verbal language
Overcome the limitation of distance	It is not very effective when the receiver is not present at the time of dialling
It takes no time to get feedback	It is less interactive
It is persuasive	Not applicable to longer and complex messages
Possible to access information without consuming too much power, time and cost	It requires being a good listener
Facilitate effective person-to-person or organization to organization information exchange etc	Since it is faster it is difficult to reply one by one to all information etc

Summary

- In business environments we spend much of our time talking and listening to colleagues and clients than writing and reading. Problems will need to be discussed, information requested, instructions given etc. To achieve co-operation and effective teamwork, good human relations skills must be developed.
- The following are characteristics of face-to-face communication: It takes different forms like private discussion, formal meetings, dealing with clients etc, requires two groups, the speaker and the listener, it is natural for the parties involved in it, it is supported by non-verbal cues to convey information like intonation of voice, facial expression, gesture, posture and body movement, and it is supplemented by verbal language.
- The other most important point that the chapter incorporate is the guidelines the caller and receiver should follow before and during telephoning. The guidelines you should use before telephoning are: Know the specific purpose of your call, Know the name and occupation (if pertinent) of the person you are calling, Consider the best time to call and others. During telephoning: Introduce yourself, Announce your name and the organization and greet the caller, Be polite avoid a barking tone, When you answer a phone call with clear pleasant voice answer promptly, usually with your name/department/ organization and greet the caller and others.
- Finally, we looked at in detail the merits and demerits of face to face and telephone conversation. Understanding and evaluating the respective advantage and disadvantage of face to face and telephone conversation enables us to choose the best way to have communication with others. It also enables the user to get prepared to any inconveniences that may result during the conversation

Exercises

1. What are the forms of face-to-face conversation?
2. Mention the characteristics of face-to-face communication.
3. List the check list for effective face to face communication.
4. Write down the merits and demerits of the face-to-face communication.
5. What do you understand by the telephonic conversation? Explain
6. What are the characteristics of telephonic conversation?

7. What are the procedures to be followed during telephonic conversation?
8. Describe the merits and demerits of telephonic conversation.

Self-Check-Questions

1. Face to face communication can take all forms except,
   (A) Private discussion (B) Formal meetings
   (C) A gossip in the lift (D) Interview
   (E) None
2. One is not the merit of face to face communication
   (A) Immediate feed back
   (B) Supplemented by verbal language
   (C) More reliable and effective
   (D) Overcome the limitation of distance
   (E) None
3. Which one is different from others
   (A) It is less interactive
   (B) It requires being a good listener
   (C) Each cannot be supplemented by verbal language.
   (D) Less concise.
   (E) None
4. All are the procedures to be followed by the caller before telephoning except,
   (A) Know the specific purpose of your call.
   (B) Know the name and occupation of a person you are calling.
   (C) Consider the best time to call.
   (D) Introduce yourself.
   (E) None.

Fill the blank space with appropriate terms

5. ______ is the life blood of our personal and business lives.
6. ________ is form of instant communication which achieves quick response but it takes imagination to use.

Write True or False for the following statements

7. In telephone conversation, you have various means of conveying information like intonation of voice, facial expressions, gestures, and posture and body movement.
8. In face to face communication the communicator does not influenced by external environment.
9. The main two roles that you can play in oral communication are listening and speaking.
10. Telephone conversation is an ear-to-ear communication.

Answers

1. E	2. D	3. D	4. D
5. Oral communication		6. Telephoning	
7. False	8. False	9. True	10. True

CHAPTER 10

Active Listening

Contents of the Chapter

- Types of Listening
- Importance of Effective Listening in Organization
- Causes of Poor Listening
- Guidelines for Effective Listening

Learning Objectives

After finishing this chapter, students should be able to:

- Define active listening
- Understand the importance of active listening for personal and organizational success
- Identify the different types of active listening
- Understand the different causes of poor listening

10.1 INTRODUCTION

Listening is a process of receiving, interpreting and reacting to the messages received from the communication sender. *Effective listening is an art of communication*, which is often taken for granted and ignored. Like any other art, listening requires to be cultivated consciously and carefully. Poor listening can be considered, as a mighty barrier to communication as listening is fundamental to all communication. It often results in losing messages due to improper functioning of communication. Listening requires conscious efforts of interpreting the sounds, grasping the meanings of the words and reacting to the message. Interpreting the sound signals is a cognitive act, which depends on the listener's knowledge of the code signals and on its attitude towards the communication sender.

Listening is defined as making an effort to hear somebody/ something. Listening is a combination of what we hear, understand and remember. We may physically pick up sound waves through our ears, evaluate the information and finally we may act based on our hearing and evaluation. Listening starts from hearing and it goes beyond hearing, since we evaluate and react based on it.

Active listening process begins when the listener pays attention to some audible sound signals and permits himself to interpret those sounds cognitively. It is a conscious process. Every human being possesses the ability to select from the sounds around him. But the selective listening is not an automatic process like that of hearing. An individual may hear many sounds but he may listen to none of them.

Effective listening is not a passive communication activity. It takes a great deal of effort and motivation to become and remain an effective listener. However, good listening is a prerequisite for success in business and the professions. Effective listening is certainly not the answer to all business problems, but it is one of the first steps leading to solutions. The case cannot be made strongly enough that organizational effectiveness is slowed down by employees and managers who do not listen well. Individual career advancement also can be impeded by poor listening. Unfortunately, poor listening is often more apparent to others than it is to the poor listener.

10.2 TYPES OF LISTENING

The three forms of listening are:

1. Content Listening

The purpose of this type of listening is to understand and retain the speaker's message. We may ask questions, but basically information flows from the speaker to receiver. Our job is to identify the key points of the message. It doesn't matter whether we agree or disagree, approve or disapprove only that we understand. Content listening enables us to understand and retain the message.

2. Critical Listening

This is meant to both understand and evaluate the meaning of the speaker's message at several levels. Critical listening generally involves interaction as we try to uncover the speaker's point of view. We are bound to evaluate the speaker's credibility as well. It enables us to evaluate the information.

3. Active/Empathic Listening

The aim of this type of listening is to understand the speaker's feelings, needs, and wants so that you can appreciate his or her point of view, regardless of whether you share that perspective by listening in an active or empathic way; you help the individual vent the emotions that prevent a dispassionate approach to the subject. Avoid the temptation to give advice. Try not to judge the individual's feelings. Just let the other person talk. Active listening is used to drown out the other person.

Regardless of whether the situation calls for content, critical, or active listening, all three types of listening can be useful in work – related situations, so it pays to learn how to apply them.

10.3 IMPORTANCE OF EFFECTIVE LISTENING IN ORGANIZATION

In business environment, three different sources of information demand effective listening: Customers, Employees, and Supervisors.

By Listening to Customers

With this the organization can learn objective information about its products or services. For example, customers can suggest desired product improvements that the research and development department may have overlooked. Listening to customers can tell us a great deal about the competition. Most companies like to compare and contrast themselves with other companies' people, information, goods and services. Customers will communicate their opinion of you, your company, and its competition if they are encouraged. It also increases sales and the level of customer satisfaction.

Listening to Employees

It is a way of showing support and acceptance, which make for a more open climate and an open climate makes employee satisfaction and productivity more likely. To show that they are listening managers' responses must communicate acceptance. "*There is a genuine working together a whole new cooperative spirit---but the most dramatic change is in the atmosphere. It was hard to cooperate when you were in a war. The change is almost too good to be true*" Joseph Leonard.

Listening to Supervisor

It is obvious that employees of an organization should listen to their supervisors. However many employees do not recognize how important it is to appear to be listening, of course, giving the appearance of listening without actually listening is unwise, but effective listening to a supervisor involves not only good listening skills but also giving a good indication that listening is taking place.

Your goal in increasing your power over your superior is essentially to create in his or her mind this image of you. You may say "This is a person who is like me in very important ways, who is loyal to me and the organization, who will help me achieve my goal, who will help me feel good in the process, this also is a person who has some expertise I value and need." Listening and responding play a key role in getting that image established.

Generally, effective listening plays crucial role for the success of the organization by increasing interpersonal communication and by creating common understanding between employees and supervisors.

10.4 CAUSES OF POOR LISTENING

People are not born with the ability to listen effectively, listening skills are learned. Unfortunately, many of us have developed poor listening habits. Poor listening can be attributed to several causes, many of them involving bad habits that can be broken.

10.4.1 Physical Barriers

Some barriers to effective listening are not directly under our control. A noisy typewriter, a duplicating machine, someone's loud voice, or a nearly vacuum cleaner could prevent us from hearing an important message. Visual distractions also pose barriers to effective listening. Concentration is the key to deal with physical barriers to listening. Other examples may be; *lighting may be too dim/bright, furniture badly positioned, room temperature too hot/cold* have effect on active listening.

10.4.2 Personal Barriers

1. Day Dreaming

It is the most common listening problem because it affects every one frequently. A speaker may mention some person or thing that triggers an association in our minds, and off we go. When we return to reality and start listening again, we may find that the third point is being discussed and we have no recollection of points one and two.

2. False Attention

Is a protection technique that everyone uses from time to time to take out the speaker when we are not really interested in what someone is saying, we pretend to listen we nod our heads and make occasional meaningless comments and eye contact to give the impression that we are listening but our mind is a million miles away from the speaker.

3. Prejudgment

Is one of the most common and difficult barriers to listening because it is an automatic process people could not operate in life without holding some assumptions. However, in new situations, these assumptions are often incorrect. In addition, some people listen defensively, viewing every comment as a personal attack. To protect their self-esteem, they may distort a message by tuning out anything that doesn't confirm their view of themselves.

4. Listen Selectively out Listening

You stay tuned out until you hear a word or phrase that gets your attention once more. The problem of without listening is that it leaves you not with a memory of what the speaker actually said but with a memory of what you think the speaker probably said.

5. Closed Mindedness

If a fault that happens, more outside the classroom especially when we are arguing we often refuse to listen to other side of argument, especially when we have already made up our mind we think there is no use in listening since we know all.

6. Personality Listening

This is natural for listeners to evaluate the speaker but our impressions should not interfere with our listening, sometimes you may be tempted to tune out. We can find different types of personal barriers that cause poor listening during the communication process and this personal barriers are more controllable than physical barriers.

7. Semantic Barriers

Refers to the different uses and meanings of words and symbols therefore, they do not necessarily have the same meaning for everyone. For your clarity of the word semantic barriers you can refer to the barriers of communication in the previous discussions.

10.5 GUIDELINES FOR EFFECTIVE LISTENING

We can improve our listening ability by becoming more aware of the practices that distinguish good listeners from bad listeners:

- Fight distractions by closing doors, turning off radios or televisions, and moving closer to the speaker.
- Depersonalize your listening so that you decrease the emotional impact of what is being said and are better able to hold your rebuttal until you have heard the total message.
- Listen for concepts and key ideas as well as for facts and know the difference between fact and principle, idea and example and evidence and argument
- Stay a head of the speaker by anticipating what will be said next and by thinking about what has already been said.
- Look for unspoken messages often the speaker's tone of voice or expressions will reveal more than the words themselves.
- Keep an open mind by asking questions that clarify understanding, reserve judgment until the speaker has finished.
- Evaluate and criticize the content, not the speaker.
- Provide feedback, let the speaker know you are with him or her, maintain eye contact, provide appropriate facial expressions.
- Take meaningful notes that are brief and to the point.

One way to assess your listening skills is to pay attention to how you listen when someone else is talking, are you really hearing what is said, or are you mentally rehearsing how you will respond? Above all try to be open to the information that will lead to higher quality decisions, and try to accept the feelings that will build understanding and mutual respect. Becoming a good listener will help you in many business situations especially those that are emotionally laden and difficult.

TIPS

Some Do's for the Listeners

- Keep quiet while listening.
- Focus on what the speaker says rather than on his/her looks.
- Control and screen out the distractions.
- Show interest in the speaker.

- Be friendly and patient towards the speaker.
- Listen first and take notes afterwards.
- Look for the main theme and main ideas.
- Let the speaker finish whatever he/she has to say without interrupting him/her.
- Find an area of interest in the speech; look interested in the speech and act interested in listening.
- Try to repeat the key-ideas during the slow and long speeches.
- Avoid pondering on a single point.
- Keep your mind open to every subject and speaker.
- Choose a quiet place to listen, if possible.
- Arrive early at the place of a seminar, lecture and meeting.
- Empathize with the speaker and try to understand his/her opinions, views and values.
- Try to probe the emotions and feelings of the speaker.
- Seek out difficult speech presentations to challenge your listening skills.
- Observe the non-verbal signals, the body movements, facial expressions and gestures.
- Try to look into the eyes of the speaker.
- Try to relate the speaker's message with your personal experience.
- Try to evaluate the speaker's message objectively.
- Try to accept criticism without losing your temper.
- Communicate feedback to the speaker. Ask questions which may encourage the speaker.

Summary

- Listening is defined as making an effort to hear some body/something. Listening is a combination of what we hear, understand and remember.

- Effective listening is not a passive communication activity. It takes a great deal of effort and motivation to become and remain an effective listener.
- Organizational effectiveness is highly affected by the listening ability of managers and employees. Individual's career advancement also can be impeded by poor listening.
- The types of listening are: Content, Critical and Active listening. Critical listening is both understanding and evaluating the meaning of the speaker's message at several levels.
- Listening ability can be improved by becoming more aware of the practices that distinguish good listeners from bad. Pay attention to how you listen when someone else is talking, are you really hearing what is said or are you mentally rehearsing how you will respond? Try to be open to the information that will lead to higher quality decisions and try to accept the feelings that will build understanding and mutual respect.

Exercises

1. What do you understand by listening?
2. Explain the various types of listening.
3. What is the importance of effective listening for an organization?
4. Mention the common causes of poor listening.
5. Point out the guidelines for making listening effective.

Self-Check Question

1. Which of the following is not one of the characteristics of an active listener?
   (A) He/she tries to both understand and evaluate the meaning of the speaker's message
   (B) He /she will draw the implications of the message to him/her while the speaker is giving a speech
   (C) He/she will evaluate the logic and the validity of the conclusions of the speech
   (D) He/she tries to understand the feelings of the speaker, regardless of whether he/she shares that perspective

(E) He/she evaluates the speaker's credibility while listening to his/her speech.

2. Effective listening is made, not born

(A) True (B) False

3. A noisy machine distracting attention while a supervisor tries to communicate with his/her subordinate is ________________ barrier.

(A) Physical (B) Semantic
(C) Personal (D) Language

4. The word "burn it" may mean "put it on fire", the same word may stand for "get a copy of it." This could be ________________ type of barrier.

(A) Personal (B) Physical
(C) Semantic (D) Psychological

5. Which one of the following communication barriers can be overcome by concentration?

(A) Physiological barrier (B) Cultural barriers
(C) Semantic barriers (D) Environmental interference
(E) None of the above

Answers

1. D 2. A 3. A 4. C 5. D

CHAPTER 11

Interview

Contents of the Chapter

- Definition of Interview
- Planning and Conducting Interviews
- Major Types of Interview
- Guidelines for Effective Employment Interview (for the Interviewer)
- Guidelines for Effective Employment Interview (for the Interviewee)
- Telephonic Interview

Learning Objectives

After finishing this chapter, students should be able to:

- Explain what is meant by an 'interview'
- Discuss the major types of interview and their purposes
- Explain the essentials of successful interviews
- Determine the responsibilities of the interviewer and the interviewee during an employment interview
- Explain the basic organization of all types of interviews
- Know the do's and don'ts of telephonic interviews.

11.1 INTRODUCTION

Interviewing is a basic means of interactive communication. A person may come across a number of employment interviews while searching for job. A person comes across a number of training and instructional interviews in which he is trained and instructed by his job properly and efficiently. The person may be called by the supervisor for the purpose of job assessment and appraisal.

Within business, professional and governmental organizations, we have many opportunities for one-to-one communication. Much of that will be casual but a considerable amount of time will focus on purposeful two-person communication. Our work might include interviewing which is one of the dyadic (two-person) communications. The interview completes a spectrum of type of dyadic communication from intimate interactions through social communication to serious instrumental communication. All are settings of dyadic communication but each is different from the other in terms of purpose and salient variables. So, the interview can be viewed as a form of dyadic where persons meet with a preconceived purpose and both of whom speak and listen to each other from time to time.

11.2 DEFINITION OF INTERVIEW

The word 'interview' refers to "all types of planned, face-to-face encounters in which at least one of the participants has a specific objective in mind" – *Cheryl Hamilton and Cordell Parker.*

Interviewing, according to this definition, includes gathering information, appraising employee's performance, settling grievances and many other interactions which are or at least going to be a part of your work life.

"Interview is a two party communication in which at least one person has a specific, serious purpose".—*Ronald B. Adler & Jeanne Marquardt Elmhorst*

This definition makes it clear that interviewing is a special kind of conversation, differing from other types in several ways. Most importantly, interview is always purposeful. Unlike other spontaneous conversations, an interview includes at least one participant who has a serious, predetermined reason for being there. Interviews are also more structured than most conversations.

11.3 PLANNING AND CONDUCTING INTERVIEWS

Before meeting for an interview, both the interviewer and the interviewee have to make plannings and preparations. Many job interviews are failures because either the applicants or the interviewer lack the skills of planning for them.

The interviewer must have clear and detailed information about the post for which the candidates are to be interviewed. He/she should be in a position to tell the candidate the working conditions, details of job operations and other responsibilities. He/she has to make proper seating arrangement for the candidates in such a way that they may feel relaxed in the waiting room before facing the interviewer. He/she should know what type of candidate is required for the job. He/she must have the bio-data of all the candidates who might attend the interview.

Likewise, the applicants too must prepare themselves for the interview situation. He/she has to know his/her own abilities in carrying out the responsibilities of the post for which he applies. He/she has to ask himself whether he/she really desires to do that work and if it is suitable for his/her talents. Secondly, he/she has to know the organization in which he/she seeks the job. He/she has also to prepare himself/herself for the probable questions, which would be asked in the interview.

11.4 MAJOR TYPES OF INTERVIEW

There are far too many types of interview situations for us to list them all. However, the basic approach to each type is similar and they possess the same basic features as:

- *Most interviews are face-to-face interactions involving a face-to-face encounter between the interviewer and the interviewee.*
- *All effective interviews are organized into three basic steps or phases: the opening phase, the question-response phase (body of the interview) and the closing phase.*

The three major types of interview namely:

1. Employment interview
2. Employee appraisal interview and
3. Grievance interview

11.4.1 Employment Interview

The employment interview is a face-to-face encounter between prospective employee and prospective employer. This type of interview is one of the most important because in it some of the most critical organizational and personal decisions are made. The critical organizational decisions are those to be made by the organization regarding the selection of the best candidate for the job and the critical personal decisions are those made by the candidate regarding the type of job and organization for a career decision.

An employment interview is basically designed to explore how well a candidate might fit a job. This exploration works both ways: the employer explores who the right person for the job is and the candidate explores the organizations' and job's fitness with his/ her qualifications, skills and career choices.

Different types of Employment Interview can be used by organizations to discover as much as possible about applicants

Structured interview: is generally used in the screening stage. The employer controls the interview by asking a series of prepared questions in a set order. Working from the checklist, the interviewer asks the candidates each question, staying within an allotted time period, for which all answers will be recorded (noted). Although useful in gathering facts, the structured interview is generally regarded as a poor measure of an applicant's personal qualities.

Open ended interview: in contrast, the open ended interview is a less formal and unstructured interview with a relaxed format. The interviewer poses broad, open-ended questions and encourages the applicant to talk freely. This type of interview is good for bringing out an applicant's personality and is used to test professional judgment.

Group interview: this is an interview set up where several candidates are interviewed simultaneously to see how they interact. This type of interview is useful for judging interpersonal skills.

Stress interview: the stress interview is used by interviewers to see how well a candidate handles stressful situations. During a stress interview, candidate may be asked questions which are specifically designed to make them uncomfortable and to unsettle. This is a type of interview which is regarded by many managers as inappropriate or unethical.

11.4.2 Employee Appraisal Interview

Performance appraisal interviews are scheduled regularly between superior and subordinate to discuss the quality of subordinates' performance.

These interviews have several functions, including the following:

Letting the Employee know where he/she Stands

This is achieved through the feedback that employees get which includes praising good work, communicating areas that need improvement and conveying to the employee his/ her chance for development.

Developing Employee Skill

Such interview can be a chance for the employee to learn new skills. If you were a supervisor, among other roles, you should be a teacher to your subordinates. You can use such interviews to show an employee how to do a better job.

Improving Employment Relationship

Through these interviews as a supervisor, you will be able to improve your relationship with your subordinates and give the subordinate a sense of participation in the job.

Helping Management Learn the Employees' Point of View

The performance appraisal interview should incorporate a two way communication, that is, both upward (from subordinate to superior) and downward (from superior to subordinate). This can help the subordinates to express their perspectives to their supervisors.

Setting Goals for the Future

One of the results of every performance appraisal interview should be a clear idea of how both the subordinate and supervisor will behave in the future.

11.4.3 Grievance Interview

The grievance interview is any type of one-to-one encounter involving conflict and its resolution. Examples of situations leading to grievance interviews include employee-employer disputes over working hours or wages, customer-salesperson conflicts and even teacher-student conflicts. The grievance interview is unique in that emotions often run at a much higher level than in the other type of interviews. However, the basic structure of a grievance interview includes most of the same factors that operate in other interview situations. The grievance interview highly requires the interviewer to be a good listener and a problem solver.

11.5 GENERAL GUIDELINES FOR EFFECTIVE EMPLOYMENT INTERVIEW

The effectiveness of an employment interview shall be examined from two sides: from the side of the interviewer and from the side of interviewee. If we assume that a certain employment interview was successful, it would mean that the employer was able to select the best candidate who fits the job and as well the candidate was able to get the right job with the right organization. The following are some general guidelines which should be followed by both the interviewer and the interviewee to make the interview situation most successful.

It is better to set these guidelines:

- Guidelines for the interviewer
- Guidelines for the interviewee

11.5.1 Guidelines for the Interviewer

The basic organization of interviews is the same for all types. All types will have *an opening phase*, *the question-response phase* (body of interview) and *the closing phase*. At these various phases, the interviewer should follow the guidelines here under to make the interview as much effective as possible.

Plan the Opening Phase

Give the interviewee a brief orientation to the interview. Conclude the opening phase by motivating the applicant to give an honest and carefully thought out answers.

Plan the Question-Response Phase (Body of Interview)

Asking whatever question comes to mind is an extremely ineffective way to learn and remember information about the applicant. Areas that should be covered include the following:

- Past work experience
- Leadership ability
- Personality characteristics and the like.

Based on these, specific questions for each area can be framed as follows:

- At what age did you commence work?
- How many jobs have you held since you left school?

Plan the Closing Phase

The closing of an employment interview is as equally important as the opening. This is to make sure that the interviewee leaves with a positive feeling and an accurate understanding of what will happen next. Give the interviewee a chance to ask questions and thank the interviewer for his/her time and cooperation.

The Interviewer will Have more Responsibility for the Manner in which the Interview is Conducted:

(i) Determine the time and place: Prior to the interview, communicate with the interviewee regarding the time and place of interview.

(ii) Determine the environment: The nature of interview usually determines the kind of environment that the interviewer should establish. Example: select an area that is free from phone calls and other interruptions.

(iii) Organize the interview carefully: An interviewer who conducts a poorly planned interview learns very little information about the candidate during the interview. Consequently, his/her decision will be made based on "gut" reactions which often results in hiring ineffective people. Therefore, interviewer must plan and organize each phase of the interview carefully.

(iv) Ask only lawful questions: There are certain questions that interviewers cannot ask of applicants during a pre-employment interview. This is based on the belief that all persons regardless of their race, sex, national origin, religion, age and so on should be able to equally compete for a job and advance in the job market based on their educational qualifications, experience, and specific skills.

To assure this, the interview questions should be framed like in the following manner:

- All questions should be job related
- The interviewer must be able to prove that the questions asked are related to the specific job.
- The same basic questions must be asked of all applicants for the same job position.

(v) Listen carefully to the interviewee: Sometimes, an employment interviewer becomes so preoccupied with the tasks of the interview to the extent that he/she forgets to listen. But listening to the interviewee is very essential as we use the information we get through listening and this information is the basis upon which the selection decisions will be made.

(vi) Clarify and verify the interviewee's responses: even though interviewers listen carefully, they can make mistakes if they assume that they understand exactly what the interviewee means. Since the interviewer and interviewee have different frames of reference or personal differences, it is easy for each to misinterpret the other's meanings. So, when a statement is unclear, the interviewer should clarify with the interviewee's response by asking further questions. The interviewer should ask questions if he/she does not understand what the interviewee is talking about.

11.5.2 Guidelines for the Interviewee

The following are ways to make you an active participant in your employment interviews and be successful in getting the job you want to hold:

(i) Plan the initial communication with your interviewer carefully

The initial contact may take a form of a letter, resume, or a phone conversation. However, before contacting the potential interviewer by way of these methods, find out as much as you can about the organization to which you are applying. Try to talk with someone who has been working with the organization, ask for literature such as annual reports that explain the firm (organization) and its policies.

(ii) Be prepared for any type of question and interviewer

As an interviewee, you cannot always predict what type of interviewer you will face. Normally, you can expect one or combination of some types of interviewers like the unstructured interviewer and the structured interviewer.

The unstructured interviewer: Expects you to take the initiative during the interview by looking for detailed responses. He/she might ask you an open ended question like "Tell me about yourself".

The structured interviewer: Usually expects you to do the opposite of the above situation. He/she plans everything in advance and gives you little chance to be creative in your responses. This type of interviewer usually asks direct and closed ended questions and wants specific to the point answers.

(iii) Exercise your responsibility during the interview

Appearance is only a part of the first impression the interviewer forms of you. It is your responsibility to add to those impressions with your smile, a firm but gentle handshake and a good and direct eye contact.

(iv) Be prepared with the questions you want to ask the interviewer

Most interviewers will invite you to ask questions. Therefore you should be able to ask a few questions like: 'Would the company support me if I pursue my education?', 'What is the typical career path of an individual entering your organization at this level?', 'Would this position require travels?'

(v) Be prepared to follow up the interview if necessary

Most interviews end with a plan for the future action on the part of one or both of the participants. When the decision will be reached and how it will be communicated is usually specified by the interviewer.

11.6 TELEPHONIC INTERVIEW

Today, in the era of technological advancement many companies conduct phone interviews in order to determine the best qualified candidates for the vacant job position. It is important to make a great impression that leads you to an in-person interview and one step closer to landing the job.

11.6.1 Phone Interview—Do's

- Prepare for the interview by compiling a list of your strengths and weaknesses, accomplishments and answers to typical questions. Have your resume in front of you to refer to when speaking about your work experience and make sure there must be a pen and paper available to take notes.
- Be in a quiet place alone—turn off the radio, television and any other background noise that might be distracting.
- Take a moment to think about the question, and, then, respond speaking slowly and clearly.
- Smile during the phone interview to project a positive tone in your voice and your image.
- Send a thank-you note after the phone interview to repeat your interest in the position.

11.6.2 Phone Interview—Don'ts

- Eating or chewing gum or candy during the interview.
- Ramble—make sure that your answers are direct and to the point.

- Interrupt the interviewer when he or she is speaking.
- Provide too much information—keep your answers short and to the point; however, make sure to fully answer the questions.

TIPS

Interview questions

- Tell me something about yourself
- Why would we employ you?
- Why do you want to work for this organization?
- If we hire you, what changes would you make?
- What are your greatest strengths?
- What are your greatest weaknesses?
- What didn't you like about previous job you've held?
- Are there any weaknesses in your education or experience?
- Where do you want to be five years from now?
- What are your salary expectations?
- What type of position are you interested in?
- What was the toughest decision you ever had to make?
- Do you have any question about the organization or the job?

Critical thinking

What could be the possible barriers to effective listening that an interviewer might face during an employment interview?

Summary

- Interviewing is a face-to-face conversation in which at least one party has a specific and serious purpose. As such it is perhaps the most common form of planned communication. Interviewing differs from other types of conversations in its purposeful nature and its degree of structure.
- Although there are many types of interviews, the same basic approach can be used in all interviews. Therefore, you should find that the information covered in this chapter can be applied to almost any other interview

situations. All effective interviews are organized into basically the same three phases: opening phase, question-response phase and the closing phase which all require prior preparations.

- Interviewers are responsible for carefully planning and organizing the interview ahead of time; asking necessary but lawful questions; and listening carefully and respectfully to the interviewees' responses. The interviewer perhaps has the greatest responsibility for the success of the interview. Interviews that are poorly planned, poorly organized and poorly executed result in neither participants learning anything valuable about the other.
- Interviewees are also responsible for contacting their interviewer prior to the interview sessions, planning answers for possible questions, communicating effectively during the interview and following up the interview when necessary.

Exercises

1. Define interview.
2. What are the major types of interview? Discuss in detail.
3. What points should be kept in mind while planning and conducting an interview?
4. Mention different types of employment interviews.
5. What do you understand by grievance interview?
6. Mention the guidelines for effective employment interview.
7. What are the guidelines you suggest for the interviewer?
8. Suggest the guideline for the interviewee.

Self-Check Questions

Fill in the blank space with appropriate terms

1. The person who asks questions in an interview session is _________.
2. In the _________ type of interview, the interviewer expects the interviewee to take the initiative and give detailed explanations for questions raised.
3. All effective interviews are basically organized into three steps: _________, _________ and _________.

4. The type of interview which highly requires the interviewer to be a good listener and problem solver is __________.
5. __________ style of appraisal interview involves the employee's in a greater degree than the other types of interviews.

Answers

1. Interviewer
2. Unstructured
3. Opening, question-response phase, Closing
4. Grievance interview
5. Problem solving

Chapter 12

Meeting

Contents of the Chapter

- Definition
- Objectives of Meetings
- Types of Meeting
- Preparation for a Meeting
- Conducting a Meeting (the Role of the Chairperson)
- Minutes of a Meeting

Learning Objectives

After finishing this chapter, students should be able to:

- Learn about meetings and their purposes
- Discuss how to plan meetings
- Explain how to conduct (lead) a meeting
- Discuss how to keep records of a meeting (minute writing)

12.1 INTRODUCTION

The meeting with the employees is found to be very useful in building formal communication the higher-ups are to encourage the employees to talk about their constructive suggestions, job problems and needs. They are also to be encouraged to express their views on whether the management practices help the job performance or interfere with it.

Well planned and productive group communications are essential for conducting modern business, to achieve objectives and results that cannot be accomplished effectively in another way. Meetings have always taken a large part of the average manager's time. In addition the increased use of teams also means that meetings are even more frequent. Just because meetings are common doesn't mean that they are always productive. A survey by one marketing research company showed that gatherings meetings executives consider one third of the they attend to be unnecessary. So, to be productive, any type of meeting will require a good preparation from all participants in general and the chairperson in particular. The chairperson is the one who takes the responsibility for planning and conducting or leading the meeting.

The activities and discussions in the meeting can be well directed if the purpose of meeting is specific and the agenda is strictly followed. The meetings help to heighten the team spirit and assure the necessary information flow by encouraging two-way communication. The useful knowledge and experience of the employees is mutually shared during the meetings.

12.2 DEFINITIONS

"*A Business meeting is a gathering where purposive discourse occurs among three or more people who exchange information on a common topic or problem, for better understanding or for solving a problem*" (Murphy and Hildebrandt, 1991).

The key words in the above definition are: '*purposive*' '*understanding*', *and* '*solving*'.

12.2.1 Purposive

A meeting is useful when the leader and participants know the reason-"specific purpose" for a meeting.

What is your evaluation of the following memorandum announcing a meeting?

Memorandum

'*To: All academic staff*

From: Mr. Pushpak Kumar, the vice dean

Subject: Meeting on the 11th

Please join the vice dean for a discussion on invigilation duties. Hope to see you on August 11, at 3:00 in the afternoon.

You may say 'I don't know where the meeting will be held, who the other participants will be' and a number of questions might run through your head as you read the above call for a meeting. Sadly, too many meetings are called in such an imprecise manner.

12.2.2 Understanding

The word understanding in our definition suggests that learning from the information presented at a meeting is a first purpose. You will gain something if there is an effort to understand through asking questions and listening actively.

12.2.3 Solving

Solving a problem is the second and major reason for a business meeting.

12.3 OBJECTIVES OF MEETINGS

Meetings are an important setting for oral communication and used for a variety of purposes:

- To provide information to a group of people
- To report on some activity or experience
- To coordinate and arrange activities

- To obtain assistance
- To put forward ideas or grievances for decision
- To create involvement and interest

Meetings can be held for two basic purposes:

- To present information
- To help solve problems

Most of the time both purposes may occur in one meet; a part of the meeting devoted to giving information and the other devoted to problem solving.

12.4 TYPES OF MEETING

12.4.1 Informational Meeting

Informational meetings are held to disseminate information and check on the understanding of those who attend. For example, the following notice appeared in an employee bulletin:

> **Notice**
>
> *All purchasing department personnel should attend a meeting on Thursday, December 4, at 3 pm in the personnel conference room. The topic will be a discussion of the new staff categories approved by the personnel office.*

At this meeting, the staff will ask questions and understand the new categories. No problems will be solved, no recommendations for change in policy will occur; rather, each person will gain improved understanding of the issue. A usual format is to have an opening informative speech by a person highly knowledgeable on the topic followed by a discussion.

12.4.2 Suggested Solution Meetings

Here two kinds of decisions are concerned with problems and solutions. The simplest is when a manager wishes to hear about options for solving a company's problem. The scenario proceeds like this:

1. There is a feeling that a problem exists.
2. A question is phrased that seeks to get to the heart of the issue such as "what should be done to control training costs?"
3. A person or committee is assigned to investigate.
4. A meeting is called to discuss possible answers, solutions or recommendation to the question.

Here the manager and review committee listen to all points of view of attendants, comment on option and perhaps potential final solutions are discussed. But no decision is made. The meeting is informative and explanatory. A final decision may be made at a second, problem solving meeting.

12.4.3 Problem Solving Meetings

When the executive or even a committee has no adequate solution for a problem, he/she or the committee seeks suggested solutions in a problem solving meeting. The problem is presented at the beginning by either the executive or someone previously appointed to prepare a written report on it. The meeting participants suggest solutions, discuss and evaluate them and arrive at a decision on which action is to be taken. The problem solving meeting requires the most careful planning and presiding over by the leader, as well as challenging participation by those attending.

12.5 PREPARATION FOR A MEETING

Successful meetings are just like interviews, presentations, or letters: they must be well planned.

12.5.1 Planning Before Calling for a Meeting

It is incorrect to assume that one person will always call a group together. Sometimes a committee is authorized by another group which could be as high as the Board of Directors. Initial planning involves five factors:

1. Deciding on the purpose of the meeting
2. Decide who the participants should be
3. Planning the date, time and place
4. Planning on the announcement of agenda
5. Plan the physical arrangements

Deciding on the Purpose of the Meeting

First, you should decide whether the meeting should even be called at all. In one sentence you should write the problem and specific purposes. If the purpose can be better attained by telephone, letter, memo, etc, the participants should not be called together for a meeting. A good meeting topic must be timely, genuine, really important and meaningful. It must present a difficulty that is within the experience of the attendants. Also the problem should be limited adequately so that the attendants are able to solve it-at least partially- within the given time. It should be about a matter that can immediately be decided by the group or about which recommendations can be made to a higher administrative body.

Decide Who Should Participate

Many business committees have a consistent group of attendants. For instance, executive committees may comprise vice president, other committees may be made up of persons working on a given account or a finance committee may consist of members from purchasing to disbursements. Additional members are also invited to supplement the regular members' contributions or to appear to make a specific report.

Regardless of whether or not the meeting is to solve a difficult, top-level problem, the attendants should be those who can make special contribution. Usually the more difficult the problem, the smaller the group-some times five or even fewer. But in some informational meetings, hundreds may be interested and gain useful explanations.

Arrange for the Meeting Date, Time and Place

The choice of date, time and place greatly depend on the audience size and make up and the purpose of the meeting.

Announce the Agenda

An agenda is nothing but a list of topics that are to be discussed in a meeting. Most often it is the meeting leader (may be you) whom we call the chairperson, who prepares the agenda so the participants know in advance the direction of the meeting.

The announcement should be made or sent early enough to give the participants adequate time to prepare their thoughts on the matter.

Decide on the Physical Arrangements

As the last step before any meeting, you as the leader of a meeting should consider such physical arrangements as: seating, material, equipment and atmosphere.

Seating

Most likely you, as the chairperson of a meeting will arrange seating, perhaps in a circle or around a conference table or in a diamond or U-shape so that all attendants will easily be able to see each other and the chairperson.

Material, Equipment and Atmosphere

Items to consider can be chalkboards, flip sheets; microphones, projector, visual aids, drinking water, glasses, etc.

12.6 CONDUCTING A MEETING

The chairperson's attitude and efficiency-from the beginning statement through the entire discussion-are critically important for the success of the meeting. The chairperson should be well prepared, able to think and act quickly, get along with others, respect their opinion, know objectives of discussion and the reasoning process, be patient and have a sincere interest in the values of cooperative group action.

12.6.1 Begin with Appropriate Opening Statement

the chairperson should prepare his/her introducing statement before the meeting. Then, present it to the attendants beginning by stating the problem, indicating the importance of the problem, suggest issues and may use a quotation.

12.6.2 Stimulate Discussion for Solution Discovery

In general, the chairperson is expected to encourage participation from all attendants and keep the discussion moving forward. To help spark discussion on each topic, write on the board or on the overhead projector the criterions a solution should meet. List on another board the possible solutions of the problem as the participants suggest them. Ask questions and keep the participants from wandering into irrelevant paths.

Maintain an atmosphere of goodwill and cooperation throughout the meeting. If a situation becomes tense or if some members are reluctant to speak or become aggressive, apply your communication skills to bring about a common understanding and smooth discussions among the participants.

12.6.3 Understand the Roles of Participants

Attendants or participants could have various roles such as initiator, contributor, opinion seeker, information giver, contributor, recorder, energizer and the like. These can be termed as group task roles.

There are also group maintaining and building roles like encourager, harmonizer, group observer, compromiser, and follower. Knowing these various roles being played by attendants of a meeting assists the chairperson in knowing how to react, how to handle role statements made during the meeting.

12.6.4 Sort, Select, and Interpret Data for Solution Evaluation

After the chairperson lists suggested solutions on the board he/she should encourage participants and the advantage and disadvantages of each suggested course of action. Here they should be listed separately and care should be taken not to impose the chairperson's own opinions on the group if he/she wishes to participate. Encourage each group member to feel a sense of responsibility for the success of the analysis. Good listening by everyone to what others offer is extremely important. Dear learner, can you remember the importance of active listening?

12.6.5 State the Conclusion and Plan of Action

Before dismissing the meeting, you as a chairperson should review what the group has accomplished by summarizing what parts of the problem members have solved or partially solved. State the decision (conclusion) clearly and definitely. If the group arrived at various conclusions, they should be listed, preferably in order of importance. Statements should also be made on how the solution the group decided will be carried out. Appointments may be made then announced later in a memo regarding the action.

12.6.6 Follow up on the Meeting

A thorough follow-up involves the following three steps:

1. Build an Agenda for the Next Meeting

Most groups meet frequently and they rarely conclude their business in one sitting. A smart chair person plans the next meeting by noting which items need to be carried over from the preceding one, what unfinished business must be addressed?, what progress reports must be shared?, what new information should members hear?

2. Follow Up on Other Members

As a chairperson, you can be sure that the promised outcomes of a meeting usually occur if you check up on other members. If the meeting provided instructions, see whether the people who attended the meeting are actually following the steps that were outlined, check on whether they are being performed. A friendly phone call and personal remark can be used for such follow up purposes.

3. Take Care of Your Own Assignments

Most homeworks that arise out of meetings need continued attention. Don't wait until the last minute because the results will be sloppy and embarrassing.

12.7 MINUTES OF A MEETING

After the meeting, the secretary of the meeting, who attended prepares a set of minutes for distribution to all attendants and any other interested party.

Definition: *"Minutes are official records of the proceedings of a meeting which summarize what was discussed and what decisions were made"*. Generally speaking, minutes should emphasize what was done at the meeting rather than what was said by the participants.

Minutes should include the following major items:

1. Name of the organization, department or group
2. Date, time, and place of the meeting
3. Name of the members present
4. Name of any other person present as invited guest
5. Name of chairperson and (at the end) recording secretary
6. Brief summary of reports
7. Highlights of solutions presented and decisions made
8. Time of adjournment and, if announced, the date for the next meeting

The minutes should objectively summarize discussions and decisions or conclusions reached. The emotions and feelings of any member expressed during the course of discussion are not recorded. However, the names of those who contributed major points and ideas should be recorded. The minute becomes final only when it is read at the end of the meeting or in the next meeting, approved and signed by the members and chairperson. Often it is circulated beforehand and then it is conformed at the second meeting including amendments and suggestion of members, if any.

12.7.1 Producing Minutes

There are three main ways of producing minutes of a meeting:

1. Verbative minutes
2. Minutes of resolution
3. Minutes of narration

1. Verbative Minutes

These minutes are used primarily in court reporting where every thing is recorded word for word. The secretary in the courtroom types every thing said in the court by the judge, the jury, and the attorneys of both parties and witnesses. The recording is made without omitting a single word and this is what we call as a verbative minute.

2. Minutes of Resolution

In this type of minutes recording what we find is the main conclusions. Here, one does not find the discussions which took place in each topic, rather the main decisions or conclusions made based on the discussions. The exact wording of every resolution passed should be recorded.

3. Minutes of Narration

These types of minutes will be a concise summary of all discussions which took place and the conclusions that were reached.

Now we know what minutes are, the points that they should include and the different ways of recording them. Now is time to see the wording of minutes.

12.7.2 Wording of Minutes

Minutes should be written in a past tense form using a third person reported speech. (Examples- the chairman asked…., the reports were presented and ....) Go through the following examples of minutes and study the wordings and the format carefully.

Format of Writing the Minutes

Name of the company or Department, group or committee conducting the meeting:

Place of the meeting

Date and time of the meeting

A list of members present should be recorded in the following manner

Present: ________________ *(first should be name of the chairperson)*

____
____
____
________________ *(List of the names of other members in their alphabetical order.)*

Body of the Minute

Following the headings and noting the time the meeting started and ended, the body presents all major decisions reached at the meeting. All assignments of tasks to meeting members should also be included in the body part. Any additional documentation such as tables and charts submitted by the participants should not be overlooked.

The end of the Minute

Here there should be a couple of blank lines for the signature of the chairperson and the secretary who prepares the minute. Before it is being distributed the minute should be read and approved by the chairperson.

In order to give you a full picture the following is a sample of minute, where you can have a closer look at the format, the wordings including the tenses used.

Minutes of ET (executive team) meeting

September 16, 2011

Executive conference room

Present: Mr. Anubhav Bhatt (Chairperson), Mr. A. P. Bansal, Miss Pratibha Singh,

Mr.Gopal Krishnan, Mr. Rajneesh Tyagi, Also present: Mrs Sonica Goel and

Mr. Ratan Singh

Review of actions taken at September 4 meeting

1. Miss Pratibha Singh to prepare a job flow chart of a work order from clients and report to the ET group.

   Due: September 29

2. Mr. Rajneesh Tyagi to present a report on salary compensation currently offered by the company.

   Due: September 29

Minutes of September 16 meeting

1. The minutes of September 4 meeting were approved as presented.
2. Job costing and time reporting

   Mr. A. P. Bansal presented a brief report on how the new Adware system for agency-client profitability will work. An internal methods team by Mr. Ratan Singh has been established with the intent of standardizing communication with clients.
3. Training progress—tuition reimbursements

   Mr.Gopal Krishnan outlined a prolapsed tuition-reimbursements program to be offered to all full-time employees after six months of employment. He proposed that a limit of rupees 20 lac be instituted.

   Action to be taken: the ET group suggested that the proposal wait until the question of agency compensation was solved.

The chairperson suggested that a detailed report of all salary compensation be presented before a final decision was made, that the report should be completed by October 20.

The chairperson adjourned the meeting 9 pm and reminded the group that the next meeting would be held on September 29.

Respectfully submitted

Mrs Sonica Goel

Recording secretary

Reflective Activity

Read the following memo carefully. Then rewrite it, in line with the guidelines outlined above. You should craft your own memo

To: All employees of Royal manufacturing PLC

From: Managing Director

Date: 28th June, 2014

I am happy to advise you that representatives of the Board will be available next Friday 5th July to acquaint you with information about additional voluntary contributions to our existing occupational pension scheme. This will help all of you to plan for a comfortable retirement, and should take no more than a few minutes of your time. Feel free to contact my office for further details. The meeting with the Board representatives will be at 11.30 a.m. in the Boardroom. In addition, experts from our finance department will be on hand to deal with any detailed queries you may have on this issue. I hope to see you there.

SUMMARY

- Meetings are a gathering where purposive discourse occurs among three or more people who exchange information on a common topic or problem, for better understanding or for solving a problem.
- The meeting with the employees is found to be very useful in building formal communication the higher-ups are to encourage the employees to talk about their constructive suggestions, job problems and needs.
- The meetings help to heighten the team spirit and assure the necessary information flow by encouraging two-way communication.
- Two basic purposes of business meetings are: to present information and to solve problems
- Effective leadership of a meeting requires careful planning before the meeting on the date, time, place, agenda, physical arrangements and participants, and a good way of proceeding through the meeting.
- During the meeting the leader has responsibilities of beginning with an appropriate opening statement and stimulating discussion for solution discovery, evaluation and choice of action. The chairperson should also encourage opinions, clarify vague statement and maintain an atmosphere of goodwill and cooperation. The leader should also be aware of the various roles of participants and respond quickly and wisely to role statements.
- After the meeting, the chairperson's responsibilities include distributing the minutes and seeing that responsible appointments are made and that a date is set to carry out the necessary action.
- Minutes are official records of the proceedings of a meeting which summarize what was discussed and what decisions were made.
- There are three main ways of producing minutes of a meeting: Verbative minutes, Minutes of resolution, and Minutes of narration.

Self-Check Questions

1. Which one of the following type of meeting is used to disseminate information to a number of people

    (A) Informational meeting (B) Problem solving meeting

    (C) Suggested solution meeting (D) Casual meeting

    (E) None of the above

2. The decision on the physical arrangement while preparing for a meeting involves
   (A) Seating arrangements (B) Materials and equipment's
   (C) Atmosphere (D) A & C only
   (E) All
3. Following up the meeting does not involve one of the following
   (A) Building an agenda for the next meeting
   (B) Recognizing the role of participants
   (C) Following up on other members
   (D) Completing assignments
   (E) None of the above
4. _________ is an official record of the proceeding of a meeting
   (A) Minute (B) Agenda
   (C) Adjournment (D) None of the above
5. One of the following ways of recording minutes lists down every word from every participant
   (A) Minutes of resolution (B) Minutes of narration
   (C) Verbative minutes (D) All

Answers

1. A 2. D 3. B 4. A 5. C

Model answer for reflective activity

To: All employees of Royal Manufacturing PLC

From: Managing Director

Date: 28th June, 2014

Come and find out how you can plan for a more comfortable retirement by taking out additional voluntary contributions to our existing pension scheme.

Date: Friday 5th July 2014

Place: Boardroom

Time of meeting: 11.30 a.m.

CHAPTER 13

Business Letters

Contents of the Chapter

- Definitions
- Characteristics of Good Business Letters
- Conventional Parts of Business Letters
- Types of Business Letters

Learning Objectives

After completing this chapter, students will be able to:

- Define business letters and explain their purpose
- List and explain the characteristics of good business letters
- Discuss the conventional parts of business letters
- List and discuss the various types of business letters

13.1 INTRODUCTION

The concern of this chapter is the verbal symbols in written communication media that we call as ***business letters***. Making choice of symbols and channels helps to ensure effective communication. This is achieved when the intended meaning of the sender and the meaning perceived by the receiver are one and the same.

Despite the recent growth in electronic communications and the convenience of telephone, letters are still a very widely used medium of communication in businesses. They are cheap to produce and postal delivery is quick and generally reliable. They also provide both the receiver and the sender with a permanent record of what has been discussed and agreed for later reference. Letters may lack the personal touch of meetings or the immediacy of a telephone call, but when matters are relatively straight forward and there is no urgency for a decision- as is the case in most routine business-they are an effective and valuable form of communication.

Business letters are written from one business firm to another or from a business firm to an individual customer. They are the most common form of written messages used by the business to communicate with people and organizations outside the firm. Therefore, business letters are often the main means of establishing business relations with the outside world.

13.2 DEFINITIONS

- "Business letter is a communication from one person to a company or vice versa and from one company to another".
- "Business letters are purposeful internal and external medium of communication designed to communicate business messages or information between the letter producer and the reader who could be a supplier, a potential customer or another business firm."
- "Business letter is the medium used for written messages often to the persons outside the firm'.

An effective business letter is a package containing essential facts such as knowledge of business procedure, mastery of the structure of language and logical thinking.

We may write a business letter for various purposes. It could be to inform readers of specific information, to persuade others to take action, to propose an idea, and so on. Whatever the purpose we have in mind when we write business letters, there are some essential characteristics that our letter should posses to enable us communicate in the most effective way.

13.3 CHARACTERISTICS OF A GOOD BUSINESS LETTER

To compose an effective business message, we need to apply certain communication principles. They tie closely with the basic concepts of communication process and are important both for written and oral communication.

They will provide you with guidelines for the choice of content and style of presenting your message specifically adapted to the purpose of your message and the receiver of your message. We will discuss these characteristics that your letter should possess in addition to the 7 C's of effective communication:

13.3.1 Accuracy

We should make every effort for accuracy not only in the mechanical and technical details but also in references and statements, dates, spellings, (especially the names of persons or of firms), the use of language and punctuation, and argument. Be accurate in all things and it is much better to rewrite a letter than to send it out containing incorrect material.

13.3.2 Thoroughness

When we read our letter over before releasing it, we should make sure that it contains the essential points that we want covered. If we are writing a reply letter to a correspondent, be sure that our answer is comprehensive and covers questions that he/she expressed or implied.

13.3.3 Conciseness

A concise message saves time and expense for both the sender and the receiver. Conciseness, is saying what you have to say in the fewest possible words without sacrificing the other qualities of your message. It will contribute to exphasize and avoid/eliminate unnecessary words so that you can make your important ideas stand out.

13.3.4 Clarity

To write a letter that will be clear to the receiver, you must first have a definite idea of what you mean to say. If you are vague in your thoughts, how can you expect the reader to grasp it immediately? To be clear, however, does not mean that you should use many words to express an idea. It just means that you should choose and use the right words.

> *Tip: read your letter over and over again before sending it and do not be satisfied unless and until it possesses clarity.*

13.3.5 Promptness

If you cannot answer a letter promptly, acknowledge its recipients and state that you will give it your early attention. Include a courteous expression of thanks in the letter.

The following five basic steps are essential before writing a message:

- Know the purpose of the message
- Analyse your audience(reader)
- Choose the ideas to include
- Collect all the facts to back up (support) your idea
- Outline and organize your message

Know Your Purpose

The first step when you plan for communicating your message is to determine your specific purpose. For example, is it to get an immediate replacement for defective articles? Or is your main purpose to announce your firm's new location? Or to apologize for a serious error? In addition to the specific purpose of each message, all communications have an underlying general purpose- to build goodwill. For example, in a refusal or a collection letter, the purpose should be two folds- not only to refuse a request or to ask for money, but also to maintain the customers' goodwill.

Analyse Your Audience

In communication process and principles of this material, you can realize how much important it is to adapt your messages as much as possible to the recipient's views, mental filter and needs. In your letter, consider the areas on which your recipient is likely to be well informed or uninformed, pleased or displeased, negative, positive or neutral.

Choose the Ideas

With your purpose and recipient in mind, the next step you will take is to choose the ideas for your message. If you are answering a letter, you can underline the main points to discuss and jot your ideas briefly in the margin or on a memo pad. If you are writing a complex message, you can begin by listing your ideas as they come to you. Then consider what facts will be most useful for that person.

Collect All the Facts

Having determined what ideas to include, ask yourself if you need any specific facts, updated figures and the like. Be sure you know your company policies, procedures, product details if the message requires them. Perhaps you should check with your boss, colleagues, subordinates or the files for an exact percentage, name of an individual, a date, an address or a statement. Sometimes you may also need to enclose a useful brochure, table, and picture or product sample.

Outline and Organize Your Message

The order in which you present your ideas is often as important as the ideas themselves. Disorganized writing reflects disorganized, illogical thought processes or careless presentation. Having done so, you need to decide on the organization of your letter where you could have two major alternatives. You can either use a deductive or direct approach where you begin with the main ideas and present discussions next or you can use the inductive or indirect approach in which you start with the relevant statements and later present the main idea.

13.4 CONVENTIONAL PARTS OF BUSINESS LETTERS

A letter is a written message in a particular format. Properly planned, well designed and neatly typed letters contribute towards the reputation and goodwill of a business organization. The business letter mostly has eight standard parts.

They have been arranged and discussed here in their top to bottom order:

- The heading
- The date
- Inside address
- Attention line (optional)
- Salutation
- Body
- Complementary close
- Signature block

13.4.1 The Heading

The heading shows where the letter comes from. It includes the organization's name, full address and almost always a telephone number.

13.4.2 The Date

The date establishes correspondence as a matter of record and provides a reference point for future correspondence. It is typed two spaces below the last line of the letter head. It is indicated in either in the upper right-hand corner or upper left-hand corner.

Example: 2 May 2014 or May 2, 2014

Both methods are acceptable, however, the first method proceeds in the logical order of day, month and year and hence it is conventional.

Reference is a code given to the letter.

13.4.3 Inside Address

It is the name and address of the person or organization to which you are sending the letter. The full address should be written two spaces below the date and two spaces above the salutation. The name of the addressee should be correctly spelled. If the addressee has no professional title such as doctor, or professor, the traditional courtesy titles are used—Mr, Ms, Mrs.

Order of arrangement of the inside address:

1st – Person and business
2nd – Committee, group or section or other small group
3rd – Company
4th – Building
5th – P.O.Box, street address
6th – City state
7th – Country

13.4.4 The Attention Line (optional)

To ensure prompt action, sometimes a letter which is addressed to a company is marked to a particular office with in the organization. The attention line is written two spaces below the inside address and two spaces above the salutation. The attention line is usually underlined.

Example: Attention: Mr. Mulugeta Abebe
Attention: General Manager

13.4.5 Salutation

Salutation is similar to greeting. It is placed two spaces below the attention line (if there is any). In most cases, it should match the first line of the inside address. When addressing an individual, use the word dear, followed by a polite title and the name of the person and a colon. When a letter is addressed to an officer by name "Dear sir" is used. If a person has a specific title, it is written before his/her name instead of the usual sir.

Subject: *The subject of a letter gives a brief title of the message. Thus, the purpose of the subject line is to let the reader know immediately what the message is about.*

13.4.6 Body

This is the main part of the letter that contains the main message of the letter and the idea of the writer. In the first paragraph, reference to any correspondence which has already taken place, should be given. In the second, the main message should be stated. The paragraphs that follow should contain further details if necessary.

In the closing paragraph, the writer must clearly state what action he/she expects the reader to take or he/she may end the letter indicating his/her expectations, wishes or intentions. The paragraphs are not given any heading unless the letter is very long and deals with several important points.

13.4.7 Complementary Close

This is the polite way of ending a letter. It is typed two spaces below the last line of the letter (body).

Example: sincerely, cordially, faithfully, best regards….

13.4.8 Signature Area

Signature is the signed name of the writer. It is placed below the complementary close. The name of the writer is usually typed four spaces below the close line providing enough space for signature.

In the left margin the following should be included

Identification mark: identification mark is put in the left margin to identify the typist of the letter two spaces below the signature

Enclosure: if any thing is attached to the letter, it must be indicated against the enclosure line typed two spaces below the identification mark. The enclosure notation reminds the reader that material is enclosed with the letter.

Example: Enc ______________

Enclosure(s) ______________

Copy to: *Copy is used when there are other organizations or individuals are required to receive and know the message.*

The following pages will show two letter structures having two different formats which are both aimed at increasing your understanding of the discussion you have read on the conventional parts of business letters.

There are two basic and most widely used letter formats which are worth a discussion:

(a) **The full block format**: is becoming very popular format. It can be typed rapidly because none of the parts of the letter are indented as is the case in the modified block format.

Model of the Full Block Format

ARVIND TEXTILE COMPANY, MOTI PRAYAG, P.O.box 211 DEHRADUN.	Heading
21/07/2000	Date
Mr, Ms, Dr (Manager, Director, etc)	Inside address
Dear Sir, Mr___, Ms_____	Salutation
Reference part Information Purpose Conclusion	Body of the letter
Sincerely, cordially, faithfully,	Complementary close
Name of company, Signature Business title	Signature area

(b) **Modified block format:** The date, the complementary close and the signature block begins at the horizontal centre of the page.

Model of the Modiified Block Format

ARVIND TEXTILE COMPANY,
MOTI PRAYAG
P.O.box 211
DEHRADUN.
July 28, 2014

Mr, Ms, Dr

(Manager, director, etc)

Dear Sir, Mr___, Ms_____

Reference part

Information

Purpose

Conclusion

ARVIND TEXTILE COMPANY,
Sincerely, cordially, faithfully,

Name of company,
Signature

13.5 TYPES OF BUSINESS LETTERS

The following are some of the common types of business letters: Enquiry, claim, adjustment, and employment. Each one of the types has been discussed in detail in the following paragraphs.

13.5.1 Enquiry Letters

Business people periodically made routine requests for information. Those routine enquiries are neutral messages that require no persuasion, and therefore, should be written using a direct plan. The enquiries may be about a product, service, or a person. A letter of enquiry must be written so that the writer will obtain all the information necessary to make a decision about the product, service or person. If you receive such letters in the work place, consider what you or your company would want to know and ask specific questions.

An enquiry about products or services should make receiver of your message glad to respond and should end by requesting. The enquiry may include only one sentence such as requesting a catalogue or it may also have several paragraphs in which questions are asked on the following areas:

- Specifications on the size, shape, quality, quantity of product required.
- Terms of payment and the price
- Sample of the product (if necessary)
- Time required for shipment of goods
- Guarantee on the products
- Availability of supply and accessories
- Cost of installation, repair and maintenance

The following two sample letters for an enquiry and a response to the enquiry have been given. It will somehow strengthen your understanding of the above discussion. Look at the following example of an enquiry letter.

A Sample Enquiry Letter

Department of Hydraulics
Arba minch University,
Arbaminch, Ethiopia
P.O.box 21

March 26, 2014

Mr. Gemechu Abraham
Professor
Addis Ababa Science & Technology University
Addis Ababa

Dear Mr Gemechu,

I am a professor in Hydraulics department at Arbamich University organizing a seminar on management of water resources in the coming June.

Based on your experience in this area, I was wondering if you would be interested in attending. The deadline for admission is May 23. It would be a great honour to have you in attendance.

Enclosed you may please find an admission form and more information about the seminar.

With regards,

Alemayehu Yirga
Professor, AMU
Enclosures (4)

A sample of response letter for the previous letter of enquiry

Hydraulics department
Addis Ababa Science and Technology University
Addis Ababa, Ethiopia

April 2,2012

Alemayehu Yirga
Professor, AMU
Arbamich

Dear Mr Alemayehu,

Thank you very much for your letter dated 26th March.

I would be honoured to attend your symposium on the management of water resources in June. I strongly agree with the fact that your university is doing so much towards the issue and would like to be part of the effort.

I am enclosing the admission sheet sent to me, and the articles I recently published on the subject. Good luck in organizing the event. I cannot wait to be there!

Sincerely,

Mr. Gemechu Abraham
Professor, AASTU

Enclosures (8)

13.5.2 Claim Letters

A claim letter is written by the buyer to the seller seeking some type of action to correct a problem with the seller's product or service. A claim letter requests some type of adjustment. Many compliant letters would probably be more successful if they carried an implied claim that the writer wanted some adjustments to be made as a result of a poor product, service or unfair treatment, practices and so on.

Claims should be written as soon as a problem is identified because delaying unnecessarily might not only push you past the warranty date but might also raise suspicions about the validity of your claims.

While writing claim letters, you should be courteous and avoid emotional language. Your reader who becomes angry with the strong language you used in your letter will be less likely to do as you ask. Instead of using an emotional language, begin your claim letter directly telling what the problem is. Once you have identified the problem, give explanations including all possible background information such as the date, the model number, the amount and so on.

A Sample of Claim Letter

BHAWAN RETAILER
JODHPUR,
RAJASTHAN
P.O.BOX 887
March 8, 2012

Mr Ajay Garg
Marketing manager
TTY food complex,
Mumbai

Dear Mr Garg

We have ordered 4000 Kg of rice our order number BR/009/99 dated February 23, 1999. Today when the shipment arrived we checked its contents and found only 3400 Kg of packed rice out of which 65 packs were badly damaged. It seems one of the cases was not packed properly or some heavy load had been placed over it in transit.

There is a great demand for your product in the town at this time of the year and we expected to clear the whole stock during the next two months. But it appears some of our customers will have to be disappointed.

With enormous resources at your command we hope you can save the situation by sending the remaining 600 Kg of packed rice immediately by quick transit service.

Regarding the damaged packs, we want your advice. There are two alternatives: either you will allow us to sell them at reduced price in which case we shall send you the total amount realized after deducting our usual 7% commissions or permit us to return them to you at your cost for replacement.

Sincerely yours,

Yogesh Sinha
Purchasing manager

13.5.3 Adjustment Letters

An adjustment letter is written to inform the customer, or the supplier, and so on of the actions taken in response to their claim letter. So, the objective of the adjustment letter is customer satisfaction and business reputation. In writing the adjustment letter, you should consider the claims very promptly because any delay will cause further annoyance. In addition you should offer further cooperation and assurance of satisfaction to prompt goodwill and good relationship with the customer.

If the claim is unclear or unreasonable or unjust, state why you are refusing or partially accepting the claim. The overall tone of your adjustment letter should adopt a gracious and confident approach. Show confidence in the recipient's honesty and in the essential worth of your own company and its products.

Guidelines for writing an adjustment letter

- Respond promptly: your customer is already angry or upset

- Begin the letter directly, telling the reader immediately what adjustment is being made
- Adopt a courteous tone: use neutral or positive language
- If appropriate, somewhere in the letter thank the reader for writing and apologize if the customer has been severely inconvenienced or embarrassed because of your company's action.
- Provide information that re-establishes your customer's confidence in the product or your company. Be specific enough to be believable.
- Close on a positive note: include additional re-sales, sales promotions, appreciation for the reader's interest in your products, or some other strategy that implies customer satisfaction and the expectation of a continuing relationship.
- Before we wind up our discussion of adjustment letters, it would be very good for you to look at the following sample of adjustment letter in response to the previous sample claim letter.

A Sample Adjustment Letter

TTY FOOD COMPLEX,
MUMBAI
P.O.BOX 990

March 13, 2012

Purchasing section
BHAWAN RETAILER
JODHPUR,
RAJASTHAN

Attention: Mr.Yogesh Sinha, purchasing director

Dear Sir,

Thank you for your letter number BR/110/99 dated March 8, 1999. We are very sorry to learn that you have been inconvenienced owing to our mistake.

Your suggestion of quick shipment of 600 Kg of packed rice is fair and we have dispatched them today through quick transit service, as desired by you. We hope they will reach in time for you to keep the dates with your clients. We also agree to bear the transportation cost of the damaged packs. Please send them back soon.

Thank for drawing our attention to this mistake because we have again carefully examined the work of our packaging and dispatch department and introduced further checks to avoid the recurrence of such mistake.

TTY food complex assures that you will not be put in such conveniences again.

Sincerely yours,

Ajay Garg
Marketing Manager

13.5.4 Employment Letters

The employment letters' objective is to get you into an interview or written test by your prospective employer. Well planned and organized employment letters will attract the employer for more information about you which will result in you being called for an interview. In this section we will see two major parts of an employment letter. i.e. application letters and resume or curriculum vitae or bio-data which are both necessary when you apply for a job/ when you seek employment in a particular organization.

Application Letter

The purpose of a job application letter is to get an interview. If you get a job through interviews arranged by Arbaminch university placement office or through other contacts, you may not need to write such letters. However, if you wish to work for an organization that is not interviewing in your campus, or when you change jobs, you will be required to write a letter for preparation of a job interview, because the application letter is the first step where you show a specific company what you can do for it. It is a form of advertising and it should be organized like a persuasive message. In your application letter you need to stimulate your reader's interest, it must be neat, clear, polite, purposeful and accurate and technically correct.

When you write your application letter, it is better if you have some knowledge about the organization you are applying because you should be able to write about how your qualification fits into its needs. The application letter should have several paragraphs such as the opening, middle and closing paragraphs.

There are two types of application letter. These are:

- Unsolicited application letter
- In response application letter

Unsolicited application letter*:* is sent to a company for which you would like to work even though no vacancies are being advertised.

In response application letter (solicited*)* are letters written in response to an advertisement. These are sent to the company or institution only when they have announced a specific job vacancy by advertisements and called for applications.

> Both Types of Letters Should Be Accompanied By A Bio-Data, or A Resume, or Curriculum Vitae.

The opening paragraph indicates the specific position the applicant seeks, where the advertisement was seen or how the applicant came to know of the vacant position and why the application qualifies for the position.

The middle paragraph(s) of the application letter presents selling points unless these are mentioned in the opening. This paragraph should give key qualifications that indicate the applicant can do the job.

Guidelines

For writing the opening paragraph

To open letters by capturing the reader's attention in business follow suggestions given as follows.

- Present your strongest, most relevant qualifications with an explanation of how they benefit the organization
- Mention the name of a person who is well known to the reader and he/she has suggested that you to apply
- When responding to a job advertisement, identify the publication in which the advertisement appeared and briefly describe how you meet each requirement stated in the advertisement.
- Cite a publicized organizational achievement, contemplated change or new procedure or product; then link it to your desire to work for the organization.
- State that you are applying for a job, and identify the position or the type of work you seek.

For writing the middle paragraph

- Present your key qualifications for the job, highlighting what is on your resume: job-related education and training, relevant work experience and related activities, interests and qualities
- Adopt a mature and business like tone

  Back up your claims of ability by citing specific achievements in educational and work settings (or outside activities)
- Demonstrate knowledge of the organization and a desire to join it by citing its operations or trends in the organization
- Link your education, experience and personal qualifications to the job requirements.

For writing the closing paragraph

- Request for an interview at the reader's convenience
- Request a screening interview with the nearest regional representative
- State your phone number with area code and the best time to reach you
- Express appreciation for an opportunity to have an interview

The Resume (Curriculum Vitae/Bio-data)

A resume is a persuasive summary of your qualifications for employment. It is a document which you will use to sell your self in the job search process. Its purpose is to convince potential employers that they should interview you. A well designed resume will emphasise your skills, abilities, talents and experience for potential employers.

The type of resume format may depend on your preference and the employer's organization you target. It may be chronologically organized around dates of employment and education, starting with the most recent position first. It may also be functional-organized around skills in which employers are interested. The third alternative is the combination of the above two designs which includes a section on employment by dates and a section on skills.

Parts of a Resume

1. *Opening section*
   - Your name, date of birth, address(residential), telephone number
   - Job or career objectives
   - Summary of basic qualifications
2. *Education*
   - List all relevant schooling and training since high school, with most recent first
   - List the name and location of every post-secondary school you have attended with the dates you entered and left and the degrees or certificates you obtained
   - Indicate your major and minor fields in college work
   - State the numerical base for your grade point average, overall or in your major, if your average is impressive enough to the employee
   - List relevant required or elective courses in descending order or importance.
   - List any other relevant educational or training experiences such as job related seminars or workshops attended and certificates obtained

3. *Work experience*
    - List all relevant work experience, including paid employment and volunteer work
    - List full-time and part time jobs, with the most recent one first--- State the month, year you started and left each job, list the job titles and describe you functions and responsibilities briefly.

      (*N.B. Note all on-the-job accomplishments such as organization recognitions letters or money.*)
4. *Activities, honours and achievements*
    - List all relevant unpaid activities, including offices and leadership positions you have held, significant awards or scholarships not listed elsewhere, projects you have undertaken that show an ability to work with others, and publications and role in academic or professional organizations.

      N.B. Exclude mention of religious or political affiliations.
5. *Personal data*
    - Omit data that could be regarded negatively or be used to discriminate against you
    - Omit references to age if it could suggest inexperience or approaching retirement
    - List job-related interests and hobbies, especially those indicating strength, sociability, or other qualities that are desirable in the position you seek.
    - Relate aspects of your training or work experience to those of the target position
    - Outline your educational preparation for the job
    - Provide proof that you learn quickly, are a hard worker, can handle responsibilities and get along well with others.
    - Present evidence of personal qualities and work attitudes that are desirable for job performance

- If asked to state salary requirements, provide current salary or a desired salary range, and link it to the benefits of hiring you.

6. *Reference*
   - List three to five references, or offer to supply the names on request.
   - Supply names of academic, employment and professional associates—but not relatives
   - Provide a name, title, address and telephone number or each reference
   - List no names as reference unless you have that person's permission to do so.
   - Exclude you present employer if you do not want him or her to know that you are seeking another position, or add "resume submitted in confidence" at the top or bottom of the resume.

For illustration, assume that the Ethiopian Telecommunication Corporation advertised a vacancy for the post of Junior Human Resource Officer on Ethiopian Herald dated August 10, 2008. The minimum requirement for the position was a B.A degree in Business Management. The interested applicants were requested to submit their application letter within 10 working days after this announcement has been made.

Look at the following application letter and resume shown on the next page as a sample. They have been written by an applicant as a response to the above vacancy announced by Ethiopian Telecommunications Corporation.

Sample of Application Letter

Mekuria Getachew
P.O.box 3030
Addis Ababa

August 12, 2008

Ato Mesafint Fantahun
Human Resource Manager
Addis Ababa

Dear Sir,

This is response to your vacancy announcement on the Ethiopian Herald dated 10th August, 2008 for the post of Junior Human Resource Officer.

I am keenly interested to join your organization because it is such a privilege to work with you and contribute my best to your efforts to connect Ethiopia to the future.

I am qualified enough to take this opportunity because I have requisite educational background and adequate work experience.

I have studied BA in business management in Arbaminch University and graduated with high distinction. During my stay in previous organization, I learned how to organize and prepare various reports using different computer packages, assisting the director of Administration.

I recently completed a three-course sequence at Grace College on Microsoft word and power point. I learned how to apply those programs to speed up letter and report writing tasks.

I would appreciate an interview with you. If you are interested in me, please call me any afternoon between 3 and 5 PM at (0911) 73-86-94 to let me know the day and time most convenient for you.

Sincerely,
Mekuria Getachew

Sample Curriculum Vitae

CURRICULUM VITAE (C.V)

NAME: Mekuria Getachew

DATE OF BIRTH: 20th November, 1985

PLACE OF BIRTH: Awassa

ADDRESS: Addis Ababa

Tel: 0911-73-86-94

E-mail: Meduria_1985@yahoo.com

OBJECTIVE: To obtain the post of Junior Human Resource Officer

EDUCATION: BA degree in Business Management, with High Distinction, 2007,

Senior secondary school- Awassa Tabor Secondary School, 2003,

Junior Secondary School- Awassa Tabor Junior Secondary School, 1999,

Primary School-Awassa Hayk Primary School, 1995.

EXPERIENCE: Assistant Administrator, EELCO since October 10, 2007 up to present.

ACHIEVEMENTS: Have been selected the "best researcher" in management and awarded, ArbaMinch University.

SKILLS: Computer skills (Word, Excel, Power point, Access), Excellent in interpersonal communications.

LANGUAGE: Fluent in Amharic and English

HOBBIES: Reading, Writing, literature and playing guitar.

REFERENCE:

- Ato Megabi Mengistu, Dean of Faculty of Business and Economics, Arbaminch University. (Tel) 046-881-49-72
- Dr Abebe Darza, Head Of Management Department, Arbaminch University. E-mail-darza2000@gmail.com

I certify that the above mentioned information is true to the best of my knowledge.

Date

Place **Signature**

SUMMARY

- Business letters are purposeful internal and external medium of communication designed to communicate business messages or information between the letter producer and the reader who could be a supplier, a potential customer or another business firm
- There are some characteristics that your letter should possess in addition to the 7 C's of effective communication, these are: thoroughness, conciseness, clarity, promptness and accuracy.

  To communicate effectively, you should go through the following five basic steps before writing your message.
  - Know the purpose of the message
  - Analyse your audience(reader)
  - Choose the ideas to include
  - Collect all the facts to back up (support) you idea
  - Outline and organize your message
- The conventional parts of business letter are: the heading ,the date, Inside address Attention line (optional), Salutation, Body, Complementary close and the Signature block.
- There are different types of business letters, namely, Enquiry letters, Claim letters, Adjustment letters, and Employment letters (including the application letter and the resume) which all have different purposes and recipients.

Self-Check Questions

Fill in the blank space with appropriate terms

1. __________ is one of the characteristics of a good business letter represented by the timeliness or urgency of the response.
2. The letter format in which none of the parts are indented is __________.
3. The part of the business letter which shows to whom the letter is written is __________.
4. The letter which is written in response to a claim letter is __________.
5. An application letter should be accompanied by __________.

6. Look at the following business letter format.

--------A--------

--------B-------

-------C--------

------------------D---

------------E--------
-----------F----------

Question: Now indicate the part of Business Letter corresponding to each letter.

(i) A refers to____________________

(ii) B refers to____________________

(iii) C refers to____________________

(iv) D refers to____________________

(v) E refers to____________________

(vi) F refers to____________________

Answers

1. Promptness
2. Full block format
3. Inside address
4. Adjustment letter
5. CV/ resume
6. (i) Heading
   (ii) Inside address
   (iii) Salutation
   (iv) Body
   (v) Complementary
   (vi) Signature area

Chapter 14

Business Reports

Contents of the Chapter

- Definition and Meaning of Business Report
- Objectives of Business Reports
- Classification of Business Reports
- Preparation before Writing Reports
- Main Parts of the Report
- Organization and Outline of Report Body

Learning Objectives

After completing this chapter, students should be able to:

- Define what is meant by a business report
- Discuss why businesses need reports and highlight the general purposes of reports
- Identify various classifications of business reports and distinguish among them
- Identify main parts of business report
- Know how to write business reports

14.1 INTRODUCTION

To carry on efficient operations, businesses need various reports. In almost any kind of responsible business job-whether you are a management, trainee, a salesperson, an accountant, a junior executive, or a vice person, you may have to write reports. Your communication effectiveness and, often your promotion and salary increases are affected by the quality of reports you write.

This chapter is exclusively devoted to written reports. It provides overview of business reports. It includes their meaning, classifications, objectives and main parts. It discusses how to prepare, organize and outline reports.

14.2 DEFINITION AND MEANING OF BUSINESS REPORT

"A Business Report is an impartial, objective, planned presentation of facts to one or more persons for specific, significant business purpose". This means, to be classified as a business report, a report must serve some business purpose. This purpose may be to solve a problem. A business report must be specific enough to be meaningful, broad enough to take in variations found in reports.

"A Business Report can be also defined as any factual, objective document that serves a business purpose."

"A Business Report is an orderly and objective communication of factual information that serves some business purpose."

Business reports are a managerial tool intended to inform or to contribute to the decision making and problem-solving process, they must be accurate, complete and unbiased. The report facts may pertain to events, conditions, qualities, progress, results, products, problems, or suggested solutions. They may help the receivers understand a complex business situation; carry out operational or technical assignments; or plan procedures, solve problems and make policy decisions about strategic planning.

The goal in developing a report is to make the information as clear and convenient to use as possible. Because time is precious, you tell your readers what they need to know—no more, no less—and you present the information in a way that is geared to their needs.

14.3 OBJECTIVES OF BUSINESS REPORTS

Organizations use reports to provide a formal, verifiable, link among people, places and times. Some reports are used for internal communication; others are vehicles for corresponding with outsiders. Some serve as a permanent record; others solve an immediate problem or answer a passing question.

Although Business Reports Serve Hundreds of Purposes, Most Reports are Used for One of the Following General Purposes

- To present the facts in an unbiased manner
- To monitor and control operations
- To help implement policies and procedures
- To comply with legal or regulatory requirements e.g. annual report
- To document work performed for a client e.g. interim progress reports, final report
- To guide decisions on particular issues e.g. research reports, justification reports
- To obtain new business or funding, e.g. sales proposals

Each of these purposes imposes its own requirements on the report writer. If your readers need information to oversee an operation, you would present your message differently than if you were contributing a decision on a complex issue. In other words, the purpose of a report affects its form.

14.4 CLASSIFICATION OF BUSINESS REPORTS

Reports are commonly classified by who initiated the report, why it is being prepared, when it is prepared, and where it is being sent. Here are some common report classifications:

Voluntary Reports Versus Authorized Reports

Voluntary reports are prepared on your own initiative. Thus, they usually require more detail and support than **authorized reports**, which are prepared at the request of someone else. When writing a voluntary report, you give more background on the subject, and you explain your purpose more carefully. An authorized report, on the other hand, is organized to respond to the reader's request.

Routine reports versus special reports

Routine or **periodic reports** are submitted on recurring basis (daily, weekly, quarterly, annually). They require less introductory and transitional material than **special reports**, nonrecurring reports that dealwith unique situations or one-time events.

Internal Reports Versus External Report

Internal reports (used within the organization) are generally less formal than **external reports** (sent to people outside the organization).

In addition to these categories, a report can be short or long, formal or informal. Formal reports are generally long-more than ten pages-and encompass complex problems. Informal reports are generally short. However, meanings of the terms "long" and "short" vary depending upon circumstances. Short, informal reports require fewer elements in their introductions, fewer transitional devices for continuity, fewer headings and usually a more personal writing style than long, formal reports. Keep in mind that a single report may have several classifications. For instance, a monthly sales report is generally an authorized, internal, routine, informal report. Nevertheless, most reports can be placed in two broad categories:

1. Informational reports and
2. Analytical reports.

Informational reports present facts on a subject, whereas, **Analytical reports** present facts with analyses, interpretations, conclusions, and perhaps recommendations. The purpose of informational reports is to explain, whereas, analytical reports are meant to convince the audience that the conclusions and recommendations developed in the text are valid.

14.5 PREPARATION BEFORE WRITING REPORTS

Before writing a report, you need to consider the planning steps. For all reports adequate preparation before writing involves the following six important planning steps regarding purpose, reader, ideas to include, facts to collect, interpretation and organization.

14.5.1 Define the Problem, Purpose, and Scope

The first planning step is to analyze the problem involved and know the purpose of your report. Ask questions like "What is wanted?" "How much?", "Why?", "When?" Answers to those questions will help you determine your problem, purpose, scope, limitations (in time and perhaps in fund), and title of the report. Then try to write your purpose in one concise, clear sentence.

14.5.2 Consider Who Will Receive the Report

Visualizing your reader or listener and his or her needs is an extremely important step in business report preparation. Who wants (or needs) this report? Who will read it? How much detail do they prefer? What is the reader's point of view? Experience? Knowledge? Prejudice? Responsibility? Will the report be sent to several—or perhaps hundreds of—persons at the same time?

14.5.3 Determine Ideas to Include

In short reports, this third step usually involves writing down—in no particular order—any general idea you will need to develop in order to meet the report's purpose. If the report is long, a detailed working plan follows. For some reports, formulating hypotheses (Hypotheses are possible explanations or solutions for analyzing a problem) is desirable (even essential) as a basis for determining what information you will need and then you will jot down the tentative topic headings in a preliminary, tentative outline.

14.5.4 Collect Needed Material

The fourth step in report preparation is to gather needed facts thoughtfully from reliable sources. They might include primary sources (collecting data from people who are actually closer to the problem) and secondary sources (published materials).

14.5.5 Sort, Analyze and Interpret Data

In this fifth step the amount of brain work depends of course on the complexity of your research as determined by purpose and reader needs. In a short, informational report this step may take only a few minutes. In a long, analytical report based on masses of detailed data from many sources, this step may require weeks of study, arranging and analysis between the first sorting and the final interpretation of data. Your analysis and interpretations should of course be objective, free from your own personal bias (if you have any). To be honest, never omit or manipulate relevant facts, though they may contrary to your own preferences or may require a decision different from what you had expected.

Now is also the time reconsider the logic of your hypotheses and whether any main ideas in your original, tentative outline should be revised. Occasionally, after investigating your primary and secondary sources, you may find that some points in your tentative outline are not logical or possible to complete. Conversely, some areas that should have been included in the outline may have been omitted. And so you now revise, add, and delete topics where necessary.

14.5.6 Organize Data and Prepare Final Outline

After careful analysis and interpretation, you will organize the findings and make the final outline. But before preparing such an outline, you need to know what constitutes a report body and to consider various methods of organizing and outlining.

14.6 MAIN PARTS OF THE REPORT

After you have completed the six preparation steps, you turn to the main parts of the report. These usually contain three sections: prefatory parts, text (body) and supplementary parts.

14.6.1 Prefatory Parts

Although the prefatory parts are placed before the text of the report, you may not want to write them until after you have written the text. Many of these parts- such as the table of contents, list of illustrations and executive summary-are easier to prepare after the text has been completed because they directly reflect the contents. Other parts can be prepared at almost any time.

Cover

Many companies have standard covers for reports, made of heavy paper and imprinted with the company's name and logo. If your company has no standard covers, you can usually find something suitable in a good stationery store. Look for a cover that is appropriate to the subject matter, attractive, and convenient. Also, make sure it can be labeled with the report title, the writer's name (optional), and the submission date (also optional).

Think carefully about the title you put on the cover. Give your readers all the information they need: the who, what, when, where, why and how of the subject. Put a title on the cover that is informative but not too long.

The Fly and Title Page

The title fly is a plain sheet of paper with only the title of the report on it. It adds formality to a report.

The title page includes four blocks of information:

- The title of the report;
- The name, title, and address of the person, group or organization that authorized the report (usually the intended audience);
- The name, title, and address of the person, group, or organization that prepared the report;
- The date on which the report was submitted.

Letter of Authorization and Letter of Acceptance

If you were authorized in writing to prepare the report, you may want to include in your report the letter of memo of authorization (and sometimes even the letter or memo of acceptance). *The letter of authorization* (or memo of authorization) is a document requesting that a report be prepared.

The letter of acceptance (or memo of acceptance) acknowledges the assignment to conduct the study and to prepare the report. This document is rarely included in reports.

Letter of Transmittal

The letter of transmittal (or memo of transmittal) conveys your report to your audience. The letter of transmittal says what you would say if you were handing the report directly to the person who authorized it, so the style is less formal than the rest of the report. For example, the letter would use personal pronouns (you, I, and we) and conversational language. The transmittal letter usually appears right before the table of contents.

Table of Contents

The table of contents outlines the text and prefatory and supplementary parts. Be sure the headings in the table of contents match up perfectly with the headings in the text.

List of Illustrations

For simplicity's sake, some reports refer to all visual aids as illustrations or exhibits. If you have enough space on a single page, include the list of illustrations directly beneath the table of contents. Otherwise, put the list on the page after the contents page. When tables and figures are numbered separately, they should also be listed separately.

Synopsis or Executive Summary

A synopsis is a brief overview (one page or less) of a report's most important points, designed to give readers a quick preview of the contents. It is often included in long informational reports dealing with technical, professional or academic subjects and can also be called an *abstract.*

14.7 TEXT OF THE REPORT

Apart from deciding on the fundamental issues of content and organization, you must also make decisions about the design and layout of the report. The following are parts you include in your text section:

Introduction

- The introduction of a report serves a number of important functions:
- Puts the report in broader context by trying it to a problem or an assignment
- Tells readers the purpose of the report
- Previews the contents and organization of the report
- Establishes the tone of the report and the writer's relationship with the audience
- Here is list of topics to consider covering in an introduction, depending on your material and your audience:

Authorization: when, how, and by whom the report was authorized; who wrote it, and when it was submitted.

Problem/purpose: The reason for the report' existence and what is to be accomplished as a result of the report's being written.

Background: The historical conditions or factors that led up to the report.

Sources and methods: The secondary sources of information that were used and the surveys, experiments, and observations that were carried out.

Definitions: A brief introductory statement leading into a list of terms used in the report and their definitions.

Limitations: Factors affecting the quality of the report, such as a budget too small to do all the work that should have been done, an inadequate amount of time to do all the necessary research, unreliability or unavailability of data, or other conditions beyond your control.

Report organization: The organization of the report (what topics are covered and in what order), along with a rationale for following this plan.

Body

The body of the report follows the introduction. It consists of the major sections or chapters (with various levels of headings) that present, analyze, and interpret the findings gathered as part of your investigation. Restrict the body to those details necessary to prove your conclusions and recommendations.

Summary, Conclusions and Recommendations

The final section of the text of a report tells readers "what you told them." A long report generally has separate sections labelled "Summary", "Conclusions," and "Recommendations". Here is how the three differ:

Summary: The key findings of your report, paraphrased from the body and stated or listed in the order in which they appear in the body.

Conclusions: An analysis of what the findings mean. These are the answers to the questions that led to the report.

Recommendations: Opinions, based on reason and logic, about the course of action that should be taken.

14.8 SUPPLEMENTARY PARTS

Supplementary parts follow the text of the report and include the appendixes, bibliography, and index.

An appendix contains materials related to the report but not included in the text because they are too lengthy or bulky or because they lack direct relevance.

A bibliography is a list of secondary sources consulted when preparing the report. List all the secondary sources you used in the bibliography.

An index is an alphabetical list of names, places, and subjects mentioned in the report and the pages on which they occur. An index is rarely included in unpublished reports.

14.9 ORGANIZATION AND OUTLINE OF REPORT BODY

How a report is organized increases the readability of the report. The report's reader, purpose, and subject matter must be considered when you choose the organizational plan for the entire report body and the text section. Then you will need to outline the topics correctly. The two usual ways to organize a report body are by the deductive (direct) and inductive (indirect) plans. Most business reports are organized deductively because readers wish to know early the recommendation or conclusions.

Deductive Arrangement

The word "deductive", or direct, means describing up front and explananing in your report the main ideas or main recommendations before presenting detailed evidence and explanation.

In a lengthy report, readers usually prefer the deductive arrangement because it gives them an immediate picture before they delve into the mass of supporting details.

Inductive Arrangement

Here you present the explanation before the main ideas or recommendation. You present much evidence and supporting materials before arriving at the main recommendation or conclusion.

14.9.1 Ways to Organize Report Text Section

One of the most challenging tasks in report writing is to decide on the best way to organize the mass of details in the text section. You must make this decision before you prepare the final outline and, of course, before you begin writing the report. You can develop the text in one (or more) of the following ways:

1. By Criteria or Topics

This is the most common. Your main headings may be the standards, factors, solution options, benefits, or characteristics-criteria-on which a decision rests.

2. By Order of Occurrence

Agendas, minutes of meetings, convention programs, progress reports, and write-ups of events or procedures may follow this chronological arrangement.

3. By Order of Location or Space

This organization is useful for any orderly description focusing on space location of units. For example, to illustrate the political implications of a policy change, you can write about its influence in Europe, the Middle East, and the western hemisphere.

4. By Procedure or Process

While close to the chronological pattern, this method traces the steps of, say, a policy or the operations of a machine or the step- by-step procedure a bank teller might use in handling a deposit or withdrawal.

5. By Order of Importance or by Alphabetization

First present the most important ideas, events, or topics and proceed to the less important points.

6. By Order of Familiarity

Always proceed from the simple or familiar to the complex or unfamiliar, because the reader can comprehend better what is known than what is not known.

7. By Sources

This method is less desirable unless you are sure your reader is most interested in what each source revealed rather than in the criteria or other important ideas.

8. By Problem Solution

This way of organization is structured in such a manner that an initial discussion of the problem followed by a solution.

14.9.2 Methods of Outlining

After you have decided how to organize the body and the text, you will arrange the headings and subheadings in an outline. A good outline, especially for reports two or more pages long, is an essential tool and a real time -saver. It will become your guide for writing the report. In a long, formal report, it also becomes your table of contents. The outline helps you- before you write the report- to see the relationship between topics, compare proportions and headings, check for loopholes in logical order, and eliminate overlapping.

Samples of Business Report

General Report

September 16, 2013

Managing Director
XYZ Manufacturing Share Co.
Addis Ababa, Ethiopia

Dear Sir,

Subject: Report on impatience among factory Workers

This has reference to your letter no. 234/11 of September 3, 2013 in which I was asked to compile a report on the impatience now prevalent among our factory workers. I have completed my investigations, and my findings with recommendations are given in a detailed report which is enclosed.

I would be obliged if I could have your comments after you have gone through the report. If, in the course of your reading, you would like to discuss some points with me, I shall be happy to do so at any time convenient to you.

Respectfully submitted

Yours truly

Mulualem Mekonen
Manager Production

Progress report

To: Mr. Gaurav Mishra, Vice-President

From; Pritpal Singh Bhatia, Assistant Vice-President

Date: July 17, 2011

Subject: Status report on the development of a Training Program

The following outlines the status of the development of the training program I have been working on for several months.

Introduction

The purpose of this research project is to determine the need for a training program in Roshan Corporation. The project, which is being undertaken by Mr. Saurabh Arora and me, is to be completed by Jan. 1, 2012.

Summary of progress already completed

The progress that has been reported up to this point includes the following:

1. Determination of objectives of the project.
2. Definition of parameters of the project.
3. Development of an appropriate research instrument (questionnaires and interviews)

Detailed summary of progress

Since the last progress report was prepared, the following have been completed:

1. Obtained approval of the questionnaire and interview record.
2. Pilot tested the questionnaire and interview record.
3. Determined method for selecting the respondents.
4. Selected the respondents.

Nature of exceptional Progress

The project is six days behind schedule because of a strike at Prime Printing, the company we have contracted with to print the questionnaires. The strike ended Oct. 15, and we expect printed questionnaires this week.

Summary of work yet to be completed

The following work remains to be done: distribution of questionnaires, completion of interviews, analysis of data, and preparation of the final report.

Periodic Reports

To: Manish Verma, Executive Vice-President

From: Gopal Nandan, Manager, Credit Department

Date: August 10, 2012

Subject: Expenditure for the Credit Dept. for July, 2012

The expenditures you asked me to calculate for the Credit Dept. for Sept., 2012 follow:

	Beginning Balance	Ending Balance	Expense
Salaries ₹	50,000	20,000	30,000
Supplies ₹	9,000	7,000	2,000
Telephone ₹	500	200	300
Printing ₹	500	300	200

The 10 Commandments of Report Writing

1. The Reader is the most important person.
2. Keep the Report as short as possible.
3. Organize for the convenience of the Report user.
4. All references should be correct in all details.
5. The writing should be accurate, concise and unobtrusive.
6. The right diagrams with the right labels should be in the right place for the reader.
7. Summaries give the whole picture in miniature.
8. Reports should be checked for technical errors, typing errors and inconsistency.
9. The report should look as good as it is.
10. The Reader really is the most important person.

Summary

- A report is an orderly and objective communication of factual information that serves some business purpose
- The functions of Business Report include: a presentation of facts on a subject, a presentation of facts with analyses and interpretations, a presentation of facts with analyses, interpretations, conclusions, and recommendations.
- There are various types of business reports: Voluntary reports, authorized reports, Routine reports, special reports, internal reports, external report.
- Before writing a report, plan your report. For all reports adequate preparation before writing involves the following six important planning steps: purpose, reader, ideas to include, facts to collect, interpretation and organization.
- The main parts of a report are: Prefatory part, Text part and Supplementary Parts.
- The two usual ways to organize a report body are by the deductive (direct) and inductive (indirect) plans. Most business reports are organized deductively because readers wish to know early the recommendation or conclusions.
- The text of a report can be organized by using one (or more) of the following ways: By criteria or topics, By order of occurrence, By order of location or space, By procedure or process, By order of importance or by alphabetization, By order of familiarity, By sources, By problem solution.

Exercises

1. What do you mean by business report? Define it.
2. Mention the objectives of business reports.
3. Describe the classification of business reports.
4. What are the main parts of report? Explain
5. Explain the followings:
    (i) Letter of transmittal
    (ii) Deductive arrangements
    (iii) Inductive arrangements

Self-Check Questions

Write True or False for the following statements:

1. A business report is an orderly communication of factual and opinion information that serves some business purpose.
2. Authorized reports require more detail and support than voluntary reports
3. All business reports are formal.
4. A monthly sales report produced by a sales representative is generally an authorized, internal, routine, and informal report.
5. The first planning step for preparing your business report is to write down the main ideas without worrying about their orders.
6. Introduction is one of the prefatory parts in Business Report.
7. An appendix which is supplementary part, contains materials related to the report but not included in the text such as questionnaires and detailed statistical calculations.
8. The order in which you first present various evidences and supporting materials, before arriving at the main conclusion is said to be inductive arrangement.
9. In your reporting, always go from unknown to known so that you would draw attention of the reader.
10. In your reporting, first present the most important topics.

Answers

1. False	2. False	3. False	4. True
5. False	6. False	7. True	8. True
9. False	10. True		

References

1. Adler, Ronald B. and Elmhorst, J.M. 2002. Communicating at Work. 7th ed. McGraw-Hill, Boston.
2. Bovee, C.L. and Thill, J.V. 2000. *Business Communication Today*. 6th ed. Prentice Hall, New Jersey.
3. Brien o Reilly, 360 feed can change your life. *Fortune*, p-93-96, 1996.
4. Charles Redding, W. 1992. *Communication within the Organization,* Industrial Council, New York.
5. Christensen, L.T and Askegaard, S. 2001. Corporate identity and corporate image revisited. *European Journal of Marketing*, 35, 3/4, 292-315, 2001.
6. Donald, B. Simmons, The Nature of the Organizational Grapevine, *Supervisory Management*, November 1985.
7. Drucker, P. 1997. *The Organization of the Future.* Jossey-Bass Publishers, San Francisco.
8. Fernandez, F.G. and Borjas, A.E.C. 2008. The Relationship Between Information and Communication Technologies and New Organizational Forms: Reference of the Manufacturing Industry in the Area of Carabobo,. *Journal of Technology Management & Innovation* 3(4), Venezuela.
9. Garry, Gemmill. 1970. Managing Upward Communication. *Personnel Journal* 49 (February).
10. Gibson, J.W., and R.M. Hodgetts. 1991. *Organizational Communication – A Managerial Perspective.* 2nd Edition. HarperCollins Publishers, New York.

11. Hamilton, C. and Parker, C. 1987. *Communicating for Results.* 2nd ed. Wadsworth Publishing Company, Belmont.
12. Kenneth R. Mayar. 1991. The Role of Style Analyzers in Business Communication, *The Bulletin* 54 (June 91).
13. Lai, V.S. (2001). Intra organizational Communication with Intranets. *Communication of the ACM,* Vol. 44.
14. Lee, J. 1997. Leader-member exchange, the "Pelz Effect," and cooperative communication among group members. *Management Communication Quartely.*
15. Locker, Kittty O. and Kaczmarek S. K. 2001. *Business Communication.* McGraw Hill, Boston.
16. Maes. J.D, Weldy and Icenogle, M.L, 1997. Oral Communication Competency in the Workplace, *Journal of Business Communication,* January97.
17. Maureen, Weiss, Manager's Tool Kit: Tapping the Grapevine, *Across the Board,* April 1992.
18. Murphy, H.A and Hildbrandt. 1991. *Effective Business Communications.* 6th ed. McGraw Hill, New York.
19. Jo, Proctor, The path to the top, *Public relations journal,* volume 39.
20. Richmond, V.P., and J.C. McCroskey. 1992. Organizational Communication for Survival. Prentice Hall. Englewood Cliffs, NJ.
21. Schneider, B., Gunnarson, S. K. and Niles-Jolly, K. 1994. Creating the climate and culture of success. *Organizational Dynamics,* 23.
22. Taylor, H., Fieldman, G., and Altman, Y. 2008. E-mail at Work: A Cause for Concern. *Journal of Organisational Transformation and Social Change* (5: 2).
23. UNDP, Human Development Report, 2001. *Making New Technologies Work for Human Development.* Oxford Univ. Press, New York.
24. White, K.W. and E.N. Chapman. 1996. Organizational Communication – An Introduction to Communication and Human Relations Strategies. *Needham Heights,* Simon and Schuster Custom Publishing, MA.

Index

O

P

R

S

T